The Homeric Hymns

The Homeric Hymns

A VERSE TRANSLATION

by THELMA SARGENT

W · W · NORTON & COMPANY · INC ·
New York

Copyright © 1973 by W. W. Norton & Company, Inc.

FIRST EDITION

Library of Congress Cataloging in Publication Data

Homerus.

The Homeric hymns.
  I. Sargent, Thelma, tr. II. Title.
PA4025.H8S3   1973   883′.01   72–12937
ISBN 0–393–04369–X

ALL RIGHTS RESERVED
Published simultaneously in Canada
by George J. McLeod Limited, Toronto
PRINTED IN THE UNITED STATES OF AMERICA

1 2 3 4 5 6 7 8 9 0

· Contents ·

· *Foreword* ·

THE HOMERIC HYMNS are a collection of anonymous poems of varying length and quality celebrating the gods and goddesses of the Greek pantheon and composed for the most part around the seventh century B.C. They are in the oral tradition of bardic poetry, with the stately six-foot measures of dactylic hexameter, the meter of the great epics of Homer. The ancients had no hesitation in attributing the hymns to Homer. Thucydides (3.104), possibly because of the autobiographical reference to a blind bard from Chios in the Delian Apollo (3a.172–73), comes right out with it, quoting "Homer" on the Delian games. Pausanias, too, though he cites other islands that claim the great poet as their own, refers unequivocally to "the hymns of Homer" (9.30.12). Even in Shelley's time, there was evidently no doubt; his translation of Hermes (4) is entitled "Homer's Hymn to Mercury." But today it is generally accepted that the hymns are not the work of Homer but were composed at a later date by a number of poets, whose identity has been lost in the misty past. For a while one Cynaithos of Chios (ca. 500 B.C.) was credited with the Delian Apollo on the authority of a scholiast on Pindar, but the date—a mere half century before Thucydides—is much too late. At any rate, whoever he was, the author of the Delian Apollo was a very fine poet indeed, second only to the creator of the hymn to Demeter (2).

The Delian Apollo (3a) and Aphrodite (5) are thought to be the earliest of the hymns, probably dating back to the eighth century. The Pythian Apollo (3b), like Demeter (2) and the majority of the hymns, is placed in the seventh century, Pan (19) in the fifth. Ares (8) is thought to be very late—of the Hellenistic period, or perhaps even as late as the fifth century A.D. Certainly this short hymn has a strangely modern tone and the god of war has undergone a mighty transformation.

The form of the poems is the *prooimion*, which means "prelude" or "preface." The question is, a prelude to what? It is generally assumed that they preceded a longer recitation, but in the case of the longer narratives this seems unlikely. I wonder if they might not, instead, have been invocations such as are offered nowadays at the opening of our public ceremonies. Just as some divines are more eloquent than others and some occasions of greater importance than others, so some hymns are lengthy narratives and others barely mention the name of the god. But even the shortest ones have a salutation and a closing, like a letter or a prayer, and are therefore a self-contained artistic unit. The closing formula of twelve of the thirty-four hymns, including Demeter (2), the Pythian Apollo (3b), and Hermes (4)—the three long hymns of later date—is "But I will remember you and also another song"; three others close with "Beginning with you, I will move on to another hymn"; and the other closings vary. But whatever the wording, it is as clearly an ending as "Amen." *

The meter is the dactylic hexameter of the epics; that is, a six-foot line, each foot composed of a long syllable followed by two short ones (−..). But there are many variations. A syllable that is long by "nature" (containing a long vowel or a diphthong), or by "position" (containing a short vowel followed by two or more consonants), may take the place of two short syllables (−−); sometimes three short syllables are elided into two; sometimes there is a fractional pause for breath; and the last foot is restricted to two syllables, the second of which may be either long or short. The first lines of the major hymns scan as follows:

Demeter	−−/−../−−/−../−../−−
Delian Apollo	−../−../−../−−/−../−.
Pythian Apollo	−../−../−−/−../−../−−
Hermes	−−/−−/−../−−/−../−.
Aphrodite	−../−../−../−−/−../−−

The rhythmic effect, over all, is not unlike that of a waltz. But although the rhythm is that of the epics, the stories themselves are simple and pleasant—light entertainment for the lighter moments of life.

Not many poets have been impelled to translate these lovely poems. While both Congreve and Shelley have translated a hymn or two and a few lesser poets have translated others, the only complete and more or less faithful translation I know of † is Hugh G. Evelyn-White's prose translation in the Loeb Classical Library series (*Hesiod, the Homeric Hymns and Homerica* [London and Cambridge, Mass., 1914; rev. ed., 1936; 1950 printing]). The most

---

* It is obvious by now that I consider "To Apollo" two hymns. In addition to what seems to me clear evidence of separate poetic mentalities of differing quality at work, lines 3a.177–78 are emphatically an ending and lines 3b.179–81 as definitely a beginning. Because the hymns are frequently cited in footnotes as the source of a mythological reference, I have not altered the numbering but have merely broken Apollo into "a" (Delian) and "b"

(Pythian) sections. For scholarly convenience, the numbering of the lines in the two hymns will forever remain consecutive.

† As this is being prepared for press, a very acceptable translation by Daryl Hine has just been published by Atheneum Publishers, New York. A translation by Charles Boer (Chicago: Swallow Press, 1971) has also appeared recently.

recent, if not the only, scholarship in the field is the exhaustive study *The Homeric Hymns,* by Thomas W. Allen, William R. Halliday, and Edward E. Sikes (Oxford, 1936); Evelyn-White acknowledges his debt to the 1904 edition of Allen and Sikes and has obviously incorporated the best of their interpretations in his text and translation in the Loeb edition cited above. Interested readers may consult these books for more detailed information, but even the existing scholarship has been considerably modified by more recent work in archeology and other related fields.

In my translation I have in general followed the text of the Loeb edition, referring to that of Thomas W. Allen (*Homeri opera,* vol. 5 [Oxford, 1912; 1961 printing]) here and there along the way when questions arose, as they often did.

I have adopted a hybrid system of transliteration for the Greek names. Where the Latin form is the one familiar to the average reader of English poetry (Olympus, Phoebus, Calypso), I have used that form. Otherwise, I have used the Greek form. However, because the letter *k* has a foreign look in English, and because *c* is hard before consonants and the vowels *a, o,* and *u* anyway, I have used *c* in all cases except "Knossos" (but, inconsistently, "Crete"). That is the spelling familiar to twentieth-century tourists, who, though not usually schooled in the classics, do get around.

Faced with dactylic hexameter, every translator has to decide for himself how he will render it in English. Some poets settle for iambic pentameter, probably the easiest rhythm of all in our language, the meter of the sonnet and of Shakespeare's plays, and, unless we watch out, the rhythm into which much of our speech naturally falls ("I mailed the letter on my way to work"). Some favor a longer, seven-foot line, iambic or otherwise, but despite its appearance, it invariably breaks down in reading to the jingly ballad rhythm of alternate four- and three-foot lines ("And this was odd because it was the middle of the night"). And some have opted for the six-stress line, whose rhythm is so subtle as to be almost indiscernible.

The difficulty is that narrative poetry is supposed to entertain—to tell a story—and dactylic hexameter is much too ponderous and portentous in tone for such a purpose. In our language it is unwieldy as well. Word order is important in English. The weak, unobtrusive little connectives "and," "but," "or," "nor," "for," so essential in a sustained narrative—and inevitable in the paratactical constructions of epic poetry—have to precede the emphatic syllable that is supposed to begin the line. Greek is more fortunate; the connectives can follow the words they connect without resulting in hopeless confusion. Moreover, in an uninflected language such as ours, modifiers must come immediately before or after the word they modify. In Greek, if metrics demand, three or four lines may separate the two—again without confusion because the case endings indicate the relationship between the words of a sentence.

I have attempted a compromise—to convey the flavor of the rhythm of the Greek, but within the more comfortable framework of the five-foot line. However, it is only a general framework. When considerations of sound or sense were more important, I have without a qualm broken my own rules. Sometimes, to relieve the monotony, I have thrown in a four-, six-, or even seven-foot line, and my "dactyls," because of the matter of word order, are amphibrachs or anapests as often as not. The rhythmic effect is the same; the waltz merely begins on the other foot.

The poems are not in the least ambiguous or obscure. They are for the most part straightforward narrative, and I have so translated them. The apparent obscurities are in reference to things foreign to our twentieth-century culture—how a temple or a Mycenaean palace was laid out, how and why the chthonic gods were invoked, how horses were yoked to a chariot, how a Greek ship was rigged. Although cities are mentioned and perfunctorily described—high, windy, sandy, well-founded (whatever that may mean), by the sea, and so on—the background of the poems is the world of nature and the pursuits of a rural population. Wealth came from the land and the food it produced rather than from factories, offices, and the stock exchange. There was manufacture and trade, but agriculture and animal husbandry were the backbone of the economy.

Cows graze, fields are plowed, barley is sown, wheat ripens and is harvested, timber is hewn. The earth is "life-giving"; sky and sea are "barren" (the sea is also deep, broad, salty, fishy, wine-dark, and loud-roaring). Heaven is starry (even by day), groves are wooded, mountains are high and forested, and forests are shadowy. The characters—especially the goddesses—are lifelike and attractive, though they redundantly see with their eyes, speak with their mouths, take with their hands, and walk with their feet. (The translator is often hard put to it to come up with suitable English equivalents for the seemingly endless variety of beautiful polysyllabic adjectives all meaning essentially "well-dressed" and simply describing the way women of the time dressed—in long, loose gowns pinned at the shoulders with ornamental brooches and secured by a sash, or girdle, low on the hips, resulting in the flowing lines of drapery we associate with "classical" art. Hera's "white" arms are really bare arms, like those of other fashionable women.) The repetitions are not necessarily significant as they would be in

English; they are in oral poetry both a memory aid and a technical device for filling out the six-foot line. They are also less conspicuous in Greek, partly because the words are longer, sometimes accounting for most of a line, partly because the endings vary according to the function of the word in the sentence.

There is hardly a noun, common or proper, that is not modified, and the modifiers are sometimes incongruous, irrelevant, even contradictory in context. These adjectives are stock descriptions, and the poet, composing aloud as he went along and needing, say, two and a half feet to fill out his line, must have just thrown in the first of an assortment of associated words of varying length that came to mind. While in some contexts *periphrōn* and *daïphrōn* may describe Persephone very well, they do not describe the young and innocent victim in the hymn to Demeter, and *kratus Argeïphontēs* —accounting neatly for nearly three of the six feet—is hardly appropriate to the newborn Hermes. Because these incongruities occur usually at the end of a line, I think they can be explained as desperate expedients under stress, and tolerantly overlooked.

I have been as painstaking in my translation as it is possible to be. I have taken very few liberties with the text, and then only for a good reason—usually to satisfy the demands of English, which differs in structure and depends for its richness of expression on verbs rather than on adjectives and adverbs; sometimes to fill out my own line, a liberty my opposite numbers would surely understand and forgive; and sometimes to clarify what the poet intended to say but didn't. (When I have been completely baffled, I have let the poet have his own way.)

I have translated *Argeïphontēs* as "slayer of Argos" throughout. I am aware that it could also mean something like "swift (or shining) appearing," and that because there is no evidence that Homer had heard of the primitive legend of Io it is nowadays usually left untranslated. But since it is agreed that Homer did not write the hymns, the argument is surely irrelevant here; any one or all of the thirty-four poets concerned could have known that Hermes was supposed to have slain the hundred-eyed monster. (On the evidence presented, he was the slayer of a tortoise and two cows, at least.) Ludicrous as it may be in connection with the infant Hermes, it has the great advantage of seeming to mean *something*, as has Shelley's "Argicide." Hawthorne's "Quicksilver" is just about perfect—witty, appropriate, and poetic—but I have scruples about borrowing.

Potnia is another troublesome word. None of the English equivalents—"lady," "mistress," "queen"—have the right vowel sound or the necessary number and arrangement of syllables to precede the names of the goddesses with which it appears, all of which contain *eta* or the *alpha-iota* combination (long *a*, *e*, or *i*). If "bothersome" had the proper worshipful connotations, it might do very well; since it has not, I have substituted other inoffensive and, I hope, appropriate adjectives.

As an epithet for Demeter, the most unwarlike of goddesses, *chrysaoros* (2.4)—"with sword of gold"—was a puzzler. If it had come at the end of the line, I could have dismissed it as an aberration for the sake of the meter, but as it appeared in the middle of the line, I assumed that the poet meant what he was saying. Resorting to symbolic language, therefore, I discovered that "gold-sworded" was really "gold-bladed," a metaphor for a stalk of ripe wheat—and what could be better for the goddess of agriculture? (In connection with Apollo, "gold-bladed" is simply more euphonious, and bypasses the homophone "sordid.")

Demeter has been slandered for too long. Whether the verb is *thēke* or *hēke* (2.253)—and I think *thēke* the more likely—I read it as simply "put." If a small baby were "dashed," "cast," or "hurled" to the stone floor of a Mycenaean palace by a tall and powerful woman, he would not be alive a few lines later (2.284) to be crying piteously (he was merely cold because the fire had gone out). Psychologically, too, the more violent verbs are improbable. Demeter is a motherly goddess, grieving over her own daughter; she has cared tenderly for this child, and however angry she may be with his mother she would do nothing to harm him. In a similar episode in Hermes (4.298), the verb is *bale*. Unlike Demeter, Apollo, a bachelor, is angry with the baby himself, but even so he would probably not have "dropped" him if the ground had not been grassy or cushioned with leaf mold or pine needles. On the whole, I think the poets are better qualified than Victorian dons to know which of the two would be the more likely to "throw" a baby.

Finally, I hope that these delightful poems, so long and so unjustly neglected, will give the reader as much pleasure as they have given the translator. Very little is known about them, and nothing at all about their creators; only the poems themselves remain to us, but "beauty is its own excuse for being." One day in Delphi I drank deeply of the cold water of inspiration of the Castalian spring (simple thirst was my reason; it was a very hot day), so perhaps Apollo is responsible not only for my having undertaken this work but for the form I have chosen. May he find my labors worthy!

New York   T. S.
October, 1972

The Homeric Hymns

· 1 · To Dionysos ·
(A Fragment)

SOME there are who say that at Dracanos, Insewn,
Some that at windy Icaros, some that at Naxos,
Others, god-born, that by the deep-eddying river of Alpheus
Semele, pregnant, bore you to Zeus who glories in thunder.
Others, lord, say you were born in Thebes, but they are all liars.
The father of men and of immortal gods gave you birth,
Far removed from mankind and in hiding from white-armed Hera.
A certain Nysa there is, a very high mountain, thick-wooded,
Far off in Phoenicia, close by the rivers of Egypt,

. . .

". . . and to her they will offer up in her temples rich gifts and many.
As these things are three, so to you always will men
Every three years sacrifice hecatombs full and unblemished."
    The son of Cronos thus spoke and, bending his dark brows, nodded.
The long ambrosial mane of the king flowed down
From his immortal head, and he caused great Olympus to tremble.
Zeus wise in counsel, so speaking, nodded his head and ordained it.
    Insewn, be gracious, you who drive women to madness;
Beginning and ending, we bards will praise you, for in no way at all
If we forget you can we recall sacred song.
Thus I bid you farewell, Dionysos, Insewn,
Semele also, your mother, by some called Thyone.

· 2 · To Demeter ·

THICK-HAIRED Demeter, dread goddess, I sing to begin,
Her and her slim-ankled daughter, whom Hades abducted,
Granted the right by far-seeing Zeus of loud thunder.
Playing apart from bounteous gold-bladed Demeter,
She with her friends, the full-breasted daughters of Ocean,
Gathered the flowers that grew in the soft, grassy meadow—
Roses and crocuses, beautiful violets, iris,
Hyacinth, too, and a magical, glowing narcissus,
Which, by the will of Zeus and as a boon to lord Hades,
Gaia sent forth as bait for the flowerlike girl.
A marvel to see was this plant for all gods and mortals:
Out of its root grew a hundred miraculous blossoms
Perfumed with headiest sweetness; all of broad heaven above
And the whole earth laughed, and the salt waves of the sea.
The girl, in astonishment, reached out with both eager hands
To take the lovely new toy. But earth of broad highways gaped wide,
And out of the cleft in the Nysan plain, driving
His immortal horses upon her, rushed lord Polydegmon,
Hades, the many-receiving, many-named son of Cronos.

He snatched her up all unwilling and carried her off
In his chariot of gold, the girl shrieking and in a shrill voice crying out
To her father, Zeus son of Cronos, highest and best.
But no one of gods or of men heard her voice, nor fruit-bearing olive,
No one but Hecate, smooth-coifed daughter of Perses,
Ever tender and thoughtful, from deep in her cave,
And Helios son of Hyperion, lord shining in splendor—
They alone heard the maiden cry out to her father.
But Zeus son of Cronos sat apart from the gods
Far off in his temple of countless prayers and entreaties
Receiving rich offerings from mortals, while, with his consent,
His brother, many-named ruler and host of the dead,
With his immortal horses carried the girl, reluctant, away.

For so long as the goddess looked upon earth and starry heaven
And the strong-flowing sea full of fish and the light of the sun,

2

And hoped still to see her dear mother and the tribes of the gods
    everlasting,
So long did hope stifle the fear in her heart.
But the peaks of the mountains rang with her immortal cries,
And the deeps of the sea, and her queenly mother heard her.
   Sharp pain stabbed at the heart of Demeter,
And her hands tore at the veiling over her ambrosial hair;
Then, tossing around her shoulders her dusky blue shawl,
She sped like an eagle in flight over dry land and water,
Frenzied, in search of her child. But no one was willing,
Either of gods or of mortals, to tell her the truth,
Nor did any prophetic bird fly to her with a true message.
Nine days queen Deo wandered over the earth,
Constantly searching, her hands holding blazing pine torches,
And in her grief touched neither ambrosia nor nectar,
Sweet to the taste, nor tumbled about in the pools.
But with the arrival of light-bringing dawn of the tenth day,
Hecate, holding a torch in her hand, came upon her,
And, straightway reporting, said a word and addressed her:
   "Noble Demeter, mistress of fruits in their season,
Of bright gifts the bestower, who of the heavenly gods or of mortals
Carried Persephone off and brought grief to your heart?
I heard the sound of her voice but saw not with my eyes
Who he was. Wholly true is this that I tell you so briefly."
   So Hecate spoke, but the daughter of lovely-haired Rhea
Said not a word in reply; with their blazing pine torches
Grasped in their hands, together they hastened away
And went to Helios, ever on watch over gods and mankind.
Standing before his chariot, the queen among goddesses spoke:
   "Helios, pity me now, a goddess, if ever truly
By word or by deed I have melted your heart and your soul.
The daughter I bore, my sweet, tender offshoot, lovely to see . . .
I heard her cry out in despair through the sky's barren waste
As if suffering harm, but with my eyes I saw nothing.
You with your beams look down out of bright heaven
Upon all things on earth and under the sea.
Truthfully tell me if you have seen my dear child,
And who, whether of gods or of mortals, by force
Carried her off against her will while parted from me."
   So she spoke, and the son of Hyperion answered:
"Daughter of lovely-haired Rhea, noble Demeter,

You shall know. Truly I honor you greatly, and pity
You in your sorrow over your slim-ankled daughter.
No other is guilty among the immortals but cloud-gathering Zeus,
Who gave the flower-fresh maiden to his own brother, Hades,
To be his wife. Hades seized her and with his horses carried the girl,
Bitterly crying, down to his shadowy underworld kingdom.
Now, goddess, leave off lamenting. Nor is there need
To nurse this terrible anger. A worthy son-in-law
Among the immortals is Hades, ruler of many,
Own brother to you and of the same seed; as to honor,
It fell to his lot in the three-way division at the beginning
To be ruler over those settling in a new realm."

So speaking, he called to his horses, wide-winged as eagles,
And under his urging they speedily bore his swift chariot away.

Anguish more piercing and savage now entered the heart of Demeter.
Enraged by perfidious, black-clouded Zeus son of Cronos,
She forsook the assembly of gods and lofty Olympus
And dwelt in the cities of men and among their rich fields,
Disguised in form a very long time. Nor did any
Who saw her, either of men or of deeply draped women,
Know her before she arrived at the palace of Celeos,
Mighty of mind, who then ruled in fragrant Eleusis.
Her heart overflowing with sorrow, she sat by the path
Near the Well of the Maiden, where housewives came to draw water,
In a shady spot (for an olive tree grew overhead),
Seeming an old woman born long ago, long past childbirth
And love gifts bestowed by flower-enwreathed Aphrodite,
Such as are nurses to children of kings who administer right,
And direct the household affairs of mansions with echoing chambers.
The daughters of Celeos, son of Eleusis, espied her
As they came to the well to draw water to fill their brass pitchers
To carry back with them to the house of their father—
Four girls like goddesses, flowers of youthful grace,
Callidice, Cleisidice, Demo, and lovely Callithoë,
Earliest born of them all. None of them knew her,
For hard are the gods for mortal beings to see,
But, standing near, with winged words they politely addressed her:

"Who are you, old woman born long ago, and where do you come from?
Why do you stay here far apart from the town,
Never approaching our houses, where women like you of great age
Live in their shadowy quarters, and younger women as well,
Who surely would welcome you kindly with both word and deed."

Thus they spoke, and the queen among goddesses answered:
"Dear children, whoever of lovely women you are,
Greetings. I will tell you my tale; not shameful for me
Would it be, since you ask, to tell you the truth.
My name is Doso, a name decreed by my mother;
From Crete, over the broad expanse of the sea,
I came by no wish of my own. Pirates by force
Carried me off all unwilling, for such was my fate.
At Thoricos they in the swift ship put in to harbor,
And there all the women, coming ashore with the men,
Made ready a meal close by the stern cables holding our ship.
But my heart had no craving for the delectable dinner,
And by stealth, hastening through the dark land,
I fled from my arrogant captors, lest they should profit
By selling me, unbought, overseas for a price.
Wandering about like a beggar, I came to this place.
I know not what land it is or what people live here.
But to you may all they who have their homes on Olympus
Grant lawful husbands, and children, whose birth is what parents desire.
In turn, have compassion on me, dear maidens, and graciously tell me
Whose house I should go to, of what man and wife, for whom
I might work at such tasks as befit an elderly woman.
I might well be employed to cradle a baby newborn
In my bent arms, or I might look after the house,
Or spread the master's bed in the innermost recess
Of the well-built chamber, or teach the women their work."

So spoke the goddess, and straightway the unmarried maiden
Callidice, shapeliest of the daughters of Celeos, answered:

"Mother, what the gods send us we mortals must patiently suffer,
However grievous our lot, for they are much stronger.
About what you ask, I will counsel you plainly, naming the men
Who hold positions of power, and who stand first
In honor among our people—the crown of our city,
Wisely guarding us with their counsel and justice.
Triptolemos, first, known as a man of discretion,
Diocles next, and Polyxenos, worthy Eumolpos,
Dolichos too, and our own illustrious father,
All of whose wives attend and manage their households.
Of them there is no one who, at the very first sight
Of your face, would shun you and turn you away from her house in
    dishonor,
But they would all welcome you gladly—for in truth you are godlike.

Stay here, if you will, while we go to the house of our father
And repeat to our mother, deeply draped Metaneira,
All you have told us straight through. Oh, if only she might
Bid you come to our home and not seek the houses of others!
Her only son, late-born to her and long prayed for—
A most welcome child—is there being raised in our comfortable
    quarters.
If you should rear him until he arrives at the threshold
Of manhood, you would be envied by any woman who saw you,
So great a reward for his care would my mother willingly give you."
    So she spoke, and Demeter, nodding, assented.
Then joyfully, filling their shiny brass pitchers with water,
They left, and lightfooted went to their father's great house.
Quickly they spoke to their mother of what they had seen and
    been told,
And as quickly she bade them summon, untried, the woman for hire.
As deer or young heifers in springtime, their stomachs sated with fodder,
Bound through the moist meadows, so they, holding in check
The folds of their swirling, shimmering garments, ran swiftly
Down the tree-shadowed road, and their long flowing hair
Danced on their shoulders like showers of bright golden blossoms.
They came upon the proud goddess close by the path
Where they had earlier parted, and then led the way
To the house of their father. She walked behind them, her heart
Heavy with sorrow. Her shawl shrouded her head,
And her blue gown rippled about her delicate feet.
    Soon they arrived at the palace of god-cherished Celeos,
And went through the airy portico to where their mother
Sat near a pillar upholding the thickly built roof,
Holding her son on her lap, a tender new twig.
The girls ran to her side, but the goddess stopped at the threshold;
Her head reached to the crossbeam, and the doorway was filled
    with her radiance.
Reverence and awe and pale terror seized Metaneira,
And she rose from her chair and urged her guest to be seated.
But Demeter, mistress of fruits in their season, of bright gifts
The bestower, cared not to sit in the richly made chair,
But stood there in silence, her beautiful eyes cast downward,
Till thoughtful Iambe, seeing her, placed for her comfort
A well-carpentered stool and threw upon it a silvery fleece.
There sat the goddess, concealing her face with her shawl.

All too long, silently grieving, she crouched on the stool,
Acknowledging no one either by word or by deed,
Saddened and still, weak from not having touched food or drink,
Ceaselessly yearning after her deeply girt daughter.
Thoughtful Iambe, seeking then to divert her,
Told jokes and jested and jeered and lightened the heart
Of the holy queen and caused her to smile and to laugh.
In later days too her jokes brightened the rites of the goddess.
Then Metaneira offered a cup filled with honey-sweet wine,
But Demeter declined with a backward tilt of her head;
It was not the custom with her, she explained, to drink sweet red wine,
And begged instead to be given a drink made of water
And barley meal blended, with pennyroyal's delicate tang.
Metaneira mixed the potion as she was directed,
And offered the cup to the goddess, Deo, great queen,
Who took it and, raising it, drank, in token of her holy rites.
Then deeply draped Metaneira began with words to address her:
  "Greetings, my lady, for well I can see your birth is not lowly,
But noble, for on your face can clearly be seen
Beauty and majesty as if of kings who administer right.
But what the gods send us we mortals must patiently suffer,
However grievous our lot, for the yoke lies on our neck.
Now you have come here, I will do for you all in my power.
Bring up this child of mine, late-born to me and unhoped-for
But greatly desired—a son granted by the immortals.
If you would rear him until he arrives at the threshold
Of manhood, you would be envied by any woman who saw you,
So rich a reward for his care would I gratefully give you."
  Bright-crowned Demeter, in turn addressing her, answered:
"Greetings also to you, my lady; may the gods bestow blessings
    upon you.
Gladly will I undertake to do as you ask
And bring up your son. Through no negligence of his old nurse
Shall the boy come to harm, I assure you, by either enchantment
Or the natural dangers that cut a plant off at the root,
For I have a powerful remedy, stronger by far than the Reaper,
And I know a lucky charm against baneful magic and witchcraft."
  So speaking, Demeter took the child with her immortal arms
To her sweet-smelling breast, and his mother rejoiced in her heart.
So, in the women's rooms of the palace, she tenderly nursed
Demophoön, beautiful son of Celeos, mighty of mind,

Born to well-draped Metaneira. The child grew in strength like a god,
But neither ate food nor was suckled at breast by his mother.
Daily the goddess, bright-crowned immortal Demeter,
Anointed the boy with ambrosia, as if he were god-born,
Breathing sweetly upon him as he lay in her lap,
And by night, unknown to his parents, she buried him like a brand
Deep in the heart of the fire. Great was their wonder
To see how he grew, for it was like meeting the gods face to face.
She would have made the boy free from old age and immortal
Had not deeply draped Metaneira, on watch one night, in her folly
Looked out from her sweet-scented chamber. She shrieked at the sight
And struck at her thighs, being afraid for her child
And chilled to her soul, and, weeping, spoke with winged words:

"My baby, Demophoön, the strange woman buries you deep
In the fire and ordains for me wailing and funeral sorrows!"

Thus, lamenting, she spoke, and the queen among goddesses
heard her.

Angered, bright-crowned Demeter reached into the fire
For the unhoped-for son Metaneira had borne in the palace
And with her immortal hands laid him down on the floor.
Her heart aseethe with resentment, she spoke to well-draped Metaneira:

"Ignorant creatures are mortals, and foolishly thoughtless,
Lacking foreknowledge of destiny, whether of good or of evil.
And you in your folly have done irreparable damage.
For—witness the oath of the gods—by the unsparing water of Styx
I would have freed your son from old age for all time
And made him immortal, besides adding undying honor.
But now he can nowise escape from death and the fates,
Yet will he forever have undying honor because
He lay on my knees and slept cradled in my bent arms.
But in the spring of his life, as the years roll around,
The sons of Eleusis for all of their days against one another
Will ever be joined in war and the dread din of battle.
I am Demeter, held in high honor, helpful
To gods and to mortals alike, and the bringer of joy.
But come, let all the people build for me a great temple,
And below it an altar, under the towering wall of the city,
Above Callichoros, up on the hill that juts out.
I myself will teach you my rites, that hereafter
In their holy observance you may propitiate me."

So speaking, the goddess resumed her own stature and aspect,

Throwing aside her guise of old age. Beauty spread all around her,
And from her blue gown drifted the lovely odor of incense;
The light of the goddess's immortal presence shone far abroad,
And the wealth of her long golden hair lay over her shoulders,
And the thickly built room blazed with a brightness as if of lightning.
Then she walked out of the palace. Straightway Metaneira's knees
    loosed in terror.
Long was she speechless, nor did she give thought to her baby,
To lift up her only, brotherless son from the floor.
But his sisters were roused by the sound of his miserable crying
And jumped down from their beds well spread with rugs. One
    picked up
The child in her arms and held him close to her heart,
Another rekindled the fire, and a third, delicate-footed,
Ran to their mother and, raising her up, led her out of her sweet-
    scented chamber.
Then, gathering gaily around the baby, they bathed him;
He struggled, resisting their loving embraces, nor was his heart
    soothed,
For less skilled were the handmaids and nurses who tended him now.
  All night long they sought, quaking with fear,
To placate the proud goddess, but with the appearance of light-bringing
    dawn
They reported to wide-ruling Celeos with unerring words
All that the goddess, bright-crowned Demeter, commanded.
He thereupon summoned his subjects far-flung to assembly,
And urged them to build a rich temple and altar nearby,
Up on the hill that juts out, in honor of thick-haired Demeter.
They were soon won by his words, and obeyed, and the temple
Was built as the goddess decreed. And the boy grew like a god.
    When the builders had finished their work and ceased from their
    labor,
They went to their homes, but golden Demeter still lingered,
Wasting, apart from all the blessed immortals,
And yearned for her deeply girt daughter. The cruelest of years
Did the goddess ordain for men on the nourishing earth.
No seed sprouted in the rich soil, for bright-crowned Demeter lay
    hidden;
Oxen in vain dragged the bent plows through the fields,
And white barley was scattered without avail on the ground.
By terrible famine she would have destroyed the whole race of men

Endowed with speech, and deprived of their glorious gifts
Of honor and sacrifice those having homes on Olympus,
Had not Zeus taken heed and pondered earth's plight in his heart.
He first sent as envoy golden-winged Iris to summon
Thick-haired Demeter, surpassingly lovely to see.
He spoke, and, obedient to black-clouded Zeus son of Cronos,
Iris on her light feet swiftly traversed the distance between,
And came to Eleusis, city fragrant with incense,
Where she found blue-robed Demeter alone in her temple.
In a clear voice, Iris with winged words addressed her:
    "Demeter, father Zeus who knows all things forever
Calls upon you to return to the tribes of the gods everlasting.
Come, let not unfulfilled be my message from Zeus."
    So, pleading, she spoke, but Demeter's heart was unmoved.
Straightway thereafter the father sent forth, one after another,
All of the blessed gods everlasting, who, severally,
Urged her return. They offered her many rich gifts
And of honors among the immortals whatever she might care to
        choose.
But no one could move her or soften her stubborn heart,
And she nursed her wrath and, unyielding, rejected their offers.
Never, she said, would she set foot on fragrant Olympus
Or send forth the fruits of the earth in their season
Until she had seen with her own eyes her fair-faced young daughter.
    Far-seeing Zeus of loud thunder, hearing her vow,
To Erebos sent off the gold-wanded slayer of Argos,
That Hermes, beguiling Hades with flattering words,
Might lead holy Persephone out of the kingdom of shadows
Into the light to be with the gods, and her mother,
Beholding her daughter once more, might cease from her wrath.
Hermes obeyed with all speed and, leaving the heights of Olympus,
Rushed eagerly downward into the depths of the earth.
He came upon Hades, lord of the realm, inside his palace,
Seated upon a couch with his unwilling bride,
A tender maiden who longed for her mother; but she, far away,
Brooded on vengeance because of the deeds of the blessed immortals.
The mighty slayer of Argos, standing by Hades, addressed him:
    "Dark-haired lord Hades, you who rule over the dead,
Father Zeus has bidden me come to lead forth
Out of Erebos to be with them the noble Persephone,
That her mother, beholding her with her eyes, may desist

From her terrible anger and wrath toward the undying gods.
For she intends that the feeble race of men born on earth
Shall perish, and hides the nourishing seed underground,
Thereby destroying the honors due the immortals.
In her terrible wrath she mingles not with the gods,
But, brooding, stays far away in her sweet-smelling temple,
Dwelling in the strong city of rocky Eleusis."

So he spoke, and Hades, lord of those under the earth,
Raised his eyebrows and smiled. He bowed to the will of Zeus,
King, and straightway urged lovely Persephone, saying:

"Persephone, go to your mother, blue-robed Demeter,
With gentleness in your heart and a steadfast spirit.
And be not beyond measure despondent, for as a husband
I am by no means unworthy among the immortals,
Being own brother to Zeus, the Olympian father.
Here you will rule over all those living and moving,
And have the greatest of honors among the immortals.
Those who offend you or slight you, who do not appease you
With sacrifice purely offered, or render you gifts
In accordance with fate, shall be punished for all time to come."

So Hades spoke, and lovely Persephone, gladdened,
Jumped up rejoicing. But he, taking thought for himself,
Secretly gave her a sweet seed of red pomegranate to eat,
Lest for all of her days she should stay far away
With her honored mother, bounteous blue-robed Demeter.
Then Hades, lord over many, led forth his immortal horses
And yoked them together before his chariot of gold,
And Persephone mounted the car and stood beside Hermes,
Mighty slayer of Argos, whose hands grasped reins and whip.
He drove away from the palace, and under his touch
The horses, flying, swiftly covered the long trackless course.
Neither sea nor the water of rivers nor grassy valleys
Nor mountaintops checked in their passage the immortal steeds,
And they cut through the thin air above as they thundered along.
At last they arrived at the temple fragrant with incense
Where bright-crowned Demeter was waiting, and Hermes halted
    the team.
Demeter, beholding them, ran to her daughter, just as
A maenad, frenzied, rushes down the forested mountain,
And at the sight of the lovely face of her mother,
Persephone, leaping down from the chariot, eagerly ran

And threw her arms around her neck and embraced her.
But while yet enfolding her child in her arms, Demeter,
Her mind at once suspicious of treachery, violently trembled,
And left off caressing her daughter and straightway addressed her:
　"Tell me, my child, did you eat any food at all down below?
Speak out, and hide nothing from me, that we may both know.
For if not, you are free of the loathsome dominion of Hades,
And may dwell with me and your father, cloud-wrapped son of Cronos,
Held in honor by all of the immortal gods everlasting.
But if you have eaten, back you must go to the depths of the earth,
There to live for a third of the span of each year,
But the other two seasons with me and the other immortals.
But when the earth blooms with all kinds of sweet-smelling flowers
In springtime, you will come up again from the kingdom
Of shadows—a wonder indeed for gods and for mortal mankind.
But tell me how he carried you off to his shadowy kingdom,
The ruthless receiver of many. What bait did he use to ensnare you?"
　Then surpassingly lovely Persephone answered her, saying:
"Indeed I will tell you unerringly, mother, all that has happened.
When the swift courier, Hermes, the bringer of luck,
Came to me from the son of Cronos my father
And the other gods of the heavens, bidden to lead me
Out of Erebos, so that, beholding me with your eyes,
You would cease from your immortal wrath and terrible anger,
I jumped up rejoicing. But Hades secretly gave me
A seed of the red pomegranate, honey-sweet food,
And forced me, reluctant, to eat it. As for the rest—
How, through the shrewd plan of the son of Cronos my father,
He came and carried me down to the depths of the earth—
I will tell you the tale from beginning to end as you ask.
We were all playing there in the lovely green meadow—
Leucippe, Phaeno, Electra, Ianthe, Melita,
Iache, Rhodea, Callirhoë, Melobosis, Tyche,
Flower-faced Ocyrhoë, Chryseis, Ianeira, Acaste,
Admete and Rhodope, Pluto, charming Calypso,
Styx and Urania, darling Galaxaura, Pallas,
Rouser of battle, and Artemis, strewer of arrows—
Playing, and with our hands picking beautiful flowers:
Modest crocuses mingled with iris and hyacinth,
Rosebuds and lilies and, wondrous to see, a narcissus
That broad earth made to grow, just like a crocus.

In delight I picked the bright blossom, but earth underneath
Gave way, and the mighty lord, the receiver of many, rushed forth
And carried me off all unwilling deep underground
In his chariot of gold, and I cried out at the top of my voice.
Deeply grieved though I am, all this that I tell you is true."

Then all day long, with their hearts in agreement, they basked
In each other's presence, embracing with love and forgetful of sorrow,
And each received joy from the other and gave joy in return.
Then smooth-coifed Hecate came and lovingly kissed
The holy child of Demeter, and the queen from that time
Served as Persephone's priestess and faithful companion.

Far-seeing Zeus of loud thunder then sent among them
As messenger lovely-haired Rhea to summon blue-robed Demeter
And lead her to the tribes of the gods, and he promised to give
Of honors among the immortals whatever she chose.
But with a nod he affirmed that her daughter must live
For a third part of the circling year in the shadowy kingdom,
But with her mother the rest of the year, and the other immortals.
So he spoke, and Rhea, obedient to Zeus,
Swiftly descended from the peaks of Olympus
And soon came to Rharos, once fertile and life-giving land,
Now lying fallow—unfruitful, all leafless, the white barley hidden
By the design of Demeter, delicate-ankled.
But soon, with the coming of spring, the grain would grow tall,
And, ripening, fill the rich furrows with tassels of gold,
To be gathered in sheaves at the harvest and bound with straw bands.
There Rhea alighted out of the sky's barren waste,
And mother and daughter, seeing each other, rejoiced in their hearts.
Then smooth-coifed Rhea spoke thus, addressing Demeter:

"Come, my child, for far-seeing Zeus of loud thunder
Summons you to the tribes of the gods, and has promised to give
Of honors among the immortals whatever you choose.
But with a nod he affirms that your daughter must live
For a third part of the circling year in the kingdom of shadows,
But the other two seasons with you and the other immortals.
So he said it shall be, and nodded his head.
Now come, my child, be persuaded, and do not beyond measure
Be angry with black-clouded Zeus son of Cronos,
But quickly send forth the life-giving fruit for mankind."

So she spoke, and bright-crowned Demeter obeyed,
And at once sent forth from the fertile land the life-giving fruit;

All of broad earth was laden with leaves and flowers.
Going then to the kings who administer right—
Triptolemos, horse-driving Diocles, mighty Eumolpos,
And Celeos, prince of his people—Demeter made known
Her holy order of service, teaching to all her most secret rites—
To Triptolemos and to Polyxenos, Diocles also—
Sacred matters to be in no way transgressed, inquired into,
Or spoken about, for great awe of the gods makes mute the voice.
Happy is he of men upon earth who has seen these wonders,
But those uninitiate, having no part in the mysteries,
Never share the same fate, but perish down in the shadows.

When she had thoroughly taught them, the queen among goddesses
Went with Persephone up to Olympus among the assembly of gods,
Where, holy and august, they dwell with Zeus who delights in loud
    thunder.
Greatly blessed of men upon earth is the mortal
These goddesses favor with love, for soon to the hearth of his house
They will send Plutos, who showers abundance on men who must die.

But come, great queen of Eleusis fragrant with incense,
Sea-girdled Paros, and rock-bound Antron; glorious Deo,
Mistress of fruits in their season, of bright gifts the bestower,
May you and your daughter, surpassingly lovely Persephone,
Graciously grant for the sake of my song a suitable stipend.
But I will remember you, goddess, and a new song as well.

· 3a · To Delian Apollo ·

I WILL remember far-shooting Apollo, nor ever forget him
 Before whom the gods in the house of Zeus tremble whenever
 he comes,
  And rise, all, in haste from their seats as he draws near and bends
his bright bow.
Leto alone remains beside Zeus who delights in loud thunder,
And with her own hands takes the bow from Apollo's strong shoulders
And unstrings it, and closes the quiver, and hangs up the weapons
On a golden peg in a pillar in the house of his father.
Then she leads him to a chair and bids him sit down,
And the father, to welcome his son, offers him nectar
In a goblet of gold. Then the other gods there
Also sit down, and lovely Leto exults
Because she gave birth to a mighty son and a bowman.
O blessed Leto, rejoice, for you bore children of splendor,
Lord Apollo and Artemis, showerer of arrows,
Her in Ortygia first, Apollo in rocky Delos,
While you leaned against the long slope of the Cynthian hill
Next to a palm tree that grew by the streams of Inopos.
  How then shall I sing of you who are in every way lauded?
For everywhere, Phoebus, the bright strains of song at you have
 been hurled,
Both on the calf-breeding mainland and in the islands.
All the high hills delight you and the tallest peaks
Of mountain ranges, and rivers that flow to the sea,
And beaches sloping down to the ocean, and the deep harbors.
Shall I tell of how first Leto bore you, a joy to mortals,
Leaning against Mount Cynthos there on the rocky
Sea-girdled island of Delos, where from all sides
Dark billows surged landward, driven by shrill-blowing winds?
For from this beginning you rule over all mortal men,
As many as Crete holds within it, and those in the confines of Athens,
The isle of Aegina, and Euboea famous for ships,
Aegae, Eiresiae, and Peparethos washed by the sea,

15

Thracian Athos, and Pelion's towering summit,
Thracian Samos,* the shadowy mountains of Ida,
Scyros, Phocaea, Autocane's pinnacling hilltop,
The well-tilled fields of Imbros, smoke-shrouded Lemnos,
Sacred Lesbos, the home of Macar son of Aeolus,
And Chios, the brightest of islands that lie in the sea;
Craggy Mimas, and Corycos' lofty summit,
Shining Claros, Aesagea's towering hill,
Watery Samos, the steep heights of Mycale,
Miletos, and Cos, pride of Meropian men,
The high slopes of Cnidos, and Carpathos fanned by fresh breezes,
Naxos, too, and Paros and rocky Rhenea—
So far did Leto travel, pregnant with the Far-Darter,
In search of a land willing to be her son's home.
But they shivered with dread: not even the richest dared receive
    Phoebus;
Until at last blessed Leto set foot upon Delos
And, straightway inquiring, addressed her, speaking winged words:
    "Delos, if you would consent to be the abode
Of my son, Phoebus Apollo, and establish here a rich temple—
For, as you will find, no one else will ever cleave to you,
Nor will you, I'd venture, be rich in cattle or sheep
Or in yield of the vine or myriad fruits of the earth.
But if you should harbor the temple home of Apollo, Far-Darter,
All men, here assembling, would come bringing hecatombs with them,
And the ineffable odor of burning would be yours forever.
Thus would you nourish those who will dwell in your land
At the hand of the stranger, for your soil is not any too fertile."
    So Leto spoke, and Delos, delighted, responded:
"Leto, most glorious daughter of powerful Coeos,
I would welcome with joy the birth of the far-shooting lord,
For truly I am of evil repute among men,
And by so befriending him should I command greater honor.
But there is a rumor that frightens me, Leto, I will not conceal it.
They say Apollo will be unbearably haughty
And lord it mightily over the immortal gods
And mortal men who live on the grain-giving land.
Much do I fear therefore in my heart and soul
Lest when he first looks upon the light of the sun
He should scorn this island, in truth very stony soil,
And with his feet overturn me and thrust me deep down

* Samothrace.

In the salt sea, where the great billows forever
Will break high over my head; then off he will go
To some other land—a place that pleases him more—
There to establish his temple and wooded groves.
And in me will the sea polyps make their abode, and the black seals
Their home, secure from all harm because I lack people.
But if you dare, goddess, swear to me a great oath
That here he will build his first most beautiful temple,
To be a seat of oracular wisdom for men,
And other temples thereafter and wooded groves
For all mankind, since surely renowned will he be."

So Delos spoke, and Leto swore the great oath of the gods:
"Bear witness now to my words, earth and broad heaven above
And the down-trickling water of Styx"—for such is the oath
Of greatest power and dread among the blessed immortals—
"Here, Delos, forever will be the fragrant altar of Phoebus
And his sacred precinct, and you will he honor far above all."

Leto thus solemnly swore, and ended the oath,
And Delos exulted and longed for the birth of the far-shooting lord.
Nine days and nine nights, pierced through by pains beyond hope,
Leto labored in childbirth. All of the goddesses,
Even the best, attended her there: Dione and Rhea,
Ichnea, Themis, and loud-wailing Amphitrite,
And the other immortal goddesses, save white-armed Hera,
Who tarried behind in the palace of Zeus the cloud-gatherer.
Eileithyia, lady of comfort to women in painful travail,
Alone had not heard of the birth. She sat apart
Under golden clouds upon the peak of Olympus,
Shrewdly detained by the cunning of snowy-armed Hera
Out of envy of lovely-haired Leto, whose destiny then
Was to bring forth to light a son both blameless and valiant.

But the others sent Iris away from the well-chosen island
To fetch Eileithyia by promising her a great necklace
Nine cubits long and strung on threads of fine gold.
They told her to summon Eileithyia aside
From Hera, white-armed, lest by words she dissuade her from coming.
Giving ear to their words, Iris, swift-footed as wind,
Set off at a run and rapidly spanned the whole distance between.
When she arrived at the seat of the gods, high Olympus,
Straightway she beckoned to Eileithyia to come to the door
And away from the palace and, speaking winged words, told her all

As she had been bidden by those having homes on Olympus.
The heart in the breast of the goddess was stirred, and they set forth
    together,
Stepping as softly as shy wood doves in their going.
When Eileithyia, lady of comfort in painful travail,
Set foot on Delos, Leto's time came and she strained to give birth.
She flung both her arms round the palm tree, her knees bearing down
Against the soft grass. Earth smiled beneath her, and into the light
Leapt Apollo, and loud cries of joy burst from all the assembled
    immortals.

   Then the goddesses bathed you, O Phoebus, purifying
You with fresh water and making you holy, and wrapped you
In swaddling clothes made of fine white cloth newly woven,
And around you tied a swaddling band fashioned of gold.
But his mother did not give suck to gold-bladed Apollo;
Themis measured out nectar and lovely ambrosia
And with her immortal hands fed him, and Leto exulted
Because she had borne a mighty son and a bowman.

   But when you had eaten the food of immortals, O Phoebus,
Gold bands had no strength to confine you nor bonds to restrain
As you struggled, panting, within them, but all the strands parted,
And straightway Phoebus Apollo spoke among the immortals:
   "Dear to me may the lyre be, and the curved bow,
And I will proclaim to mankind the infallible will of Zeus."

   So spoke Phoebus who shoots from afar, and his long hair
Tossed as he strode up and down on the earth of broad pathways,
And all the goddesses gazed upon him in wonder.
Then all Delos blossomed with gold, as the peak of a mountain
Blossoms with flowers of the woodland. She looked fondly down
On the child born of Zeus and of Leto, reflecting with joy
That the god had chosen her over the islands and mainland
To be his home, and she loved him yet more in her heart.

   Far-shooting god of the silver bow, lord Apollo,
Sometimes you strode on the rocky slopes of Mount Cynthos,
At other times ranged the islands and roamed among men.
Many temples are yours, and wooded groves,
And dear to you are all hilltops and the highest peaks
Of mountain ranges, and rivers that flow to the sea.
But mostly in Delos, O Phoebus, does joy fill your heart,
There where Ionians, trailing long tunics, gather together
With their children and excellent wives to do you honor,

Taking delight in boxing and dancing and song
In remembrance of you whenever they stage their games.
Immortal they might be called, and free from old age forever,
By one who encountered them there assembled together,
For he would remark the grace of all, and rejoice
In his soul to see the men and the beautiful women
In deeply draped gowns, and their swift ships and many possessions.
And this great wonder besides, whose fame will never perish:
The maidens of Delos attendant upon the Far-Darter.
When they have raised their voices in songs of praise first to Apollo,
Then Leto, in turn, and Artemis, showerer of arrows,
They hymn an anthem commemorating the men
And women of old, and charm the nations of people.
They know how to mimic the manner of speech of all men
And their chattering clattering tongues, and each hearer would swear
He himself had uttered the sounds, so near true is their beautiful
     singing.
   But come, may Apollo be gracious, and Artemis too!
Maidens, farewell to you all, and in time hereafter
Bear me in mind if ever someone of men upon earth,
A weary, travel-worn stranger, should come here and ask:
"O maidens, what man to you is the sweetest of singers
Who frequent this place, and whose songs give you greatest delight?"
Then all of you answer in unison, choosing felicitous words:
"A blind man who lives on the rugged island of Chios,
All of whose songs in aftertime will be known as the best."
And your own fame will we carry as far as we roam
On earth among the populous cities of men,
And all who hear will believe, for indeed it is true.
Nor will I cease to sing in praise of far-shooting Apollo,
God of the silver bow, born of lovely-haired Leto.

· 3b · To Pythian Apollo ·

LORD, to you belong Lycia and lovely Maeonia,
  And yours is Miletos, enchanting town by the side of the sea,
  But over wave-washed Delos most of all do you reign.
  And he goes on his way, the son of glorious Leto,
To rocky Pytho, playing on the strings of the hollow lyre,
And wearing immortal garments fragrant with incense, and his lyre
Under the golden plectrum gives forth a beautiful sound.
There, quick as thought, he goes from earth to Olympus,
To the palace of Zeus and to the assembly of gods,
And straightway music and singing beguile the immortals.
All the Muses together, voice answering heavenly voice,
Hymn the undying gifts of the gods and the sufferings of men,
Who, enduring so much at the hands of the gods everlasting,
Live heedless and helpless, unable to find for themselves
Either a cure for death or a bulwark against old age.
The lovely-haired Graces and imperturbable Hours,
Harmonia and Hebe and the daughter of Zeus, Aphrodite,
Dancè all together, their hands clasping the wrists of the others,
And among them dances one neither ill-favored nor puny
But tall and stately to look on and wondrous in form—
Artemis, showerer of arrows, born with Apollo.
Among them play Ares and Hermes, far-seeing slayer of Argos;
And Phoebus Apollo, stroking the strings of his lyre,
Steps high and nimbly among them, and around him radiance shines
From the gleam of his flashing feet and his fine-woven chiton.
And the great hearts of golden-haired Leto and Zeus wise in counsel
Swell with joy as they look on their son playing among the immortals.
  How then shall I sing of you who are in every way lauded?
Shall I remember you as a wooer and lover?
How you and godlike Ischys, the son of the horseman Elatos,
Went, rivals in love, to the daughter of Azan?
Or with Phorbas, blood kin of Triops, or with Ereutheus?
Or with Leucippos and also the wife of Leucippos

· · ·

One afoot and one in his chariot, but fell not behind Triops.
Or shall I tell of how, journeying over the land,
Far-shooting Apollo, you searched for a spot to establish
The very first shrine of oracular wisdom for men?
You went to Pieria first, stepping down from Olympus;
Then beyond sandy Lectos you traveled, on to the Enienes,
And through the Perrhaibians. Soon you came to Iolcos.
Then you set foot on Cenaion, in Euboea famous for ships.
And you stood on the Lelantine plain. But it pleased not your heart
There to build your temple amid wooded groves.
Then you crossed the Euripos, far-shooting Apollo,
And climbed the holy green hill, and then, traveling on,
Quickly reached Mycalesscs and grassy Teumessos.
Soon you arrived at the forest-clad dwelling of Thebe
(For no one of mortals yet lived in consecrate Thebes,
Nor were there then pathways or roads in the wheat-growing plain
That lies around Thebes, but only woodland held sway).
   Thereafter still farther you traveled, far-shooting Apollo,
Till you came to Onchestos, the beautiful grove of Poseidon.
There colts newly broken, wearied by pulling fine chariots,
Find breath again when the good charioteer jumps to earth from
     the car
And goes on his way. For a while then the colts, free
Of the hand of the driver, rattle the now empty chariot,
And if they should shake it asunder, there in the wooded grove,
Men attend to the horses, but leave the wreck leaning aslant,
For so was it ordained in the very beginning:
The drivers pray to Poseidon, but the chariot remains as his portion.
   Thereafter still farther you traveled, far-shooting Apollo,
Till you reached the fine-flowing Cephissos, whose water pours
     forth
In a fast-running stream from Lilaea. Then, crossing the river,
Onward you journeyed, Far-Worker, to Ocalea,
Multiple-towered, and thence on to grassy Haliartos.
   On you went to Telphusa, and that pleasant spot
Delighted your heart. There you thought fit to establish
Your temple and wooded groves, and you drew near and said:
   "Telphusa, here I intend to build a most beautiful temple,
A shrine of oracular wisdom for men. Here they will always
Bring me as offering hecatombs full and unblemished—
As many as live in the fertile Peloponnesos,

All they who dwell in Europe, and those from the sea-washed isles
Who come seeking truth—and I will proclaim to them all
Infallible wisdom and counsel in my rich temple."

Speaking thus, Phoebus Apollo laid down the foundations
Full-length of his temple, making it wide and exceedingly long.
Telphusa, angry at heart at the sight, spoke a word:
"Lord Phoebus, Far-Worker, a thought would I plant in your mind,
Since here you intend to build a most beautiful temple
To be a shrine of oracular wisdom for men,
Where they will always bring you hecatombs full and unblemished.
But let me speak out, and you ponder my words in your heart.
The clatter of swift-footed horses will always distress you,
And the sight of mules drinking from my sacred springs.
Too, some of the men who come here would rather admire
Chariots of ingenious construction and the prancing of swift-footed
    horses
Than your own magnificent temple and the many treasures within.
But if you will let me persuade you—for you, lord, are better
And stronger than I, and your strength is mighty indeed—
Build your temple in Crisa, under the cleft of Parnassos.
There will there be no rumble of beautiful chariots
Around your well-fashioned altar, nor the clatter of swift-footed
    horses.
But all the illustrious tribes of mankind will come
Bearing gifts to you as Iepaeon, healer,
And you will rejoice in your heart and receive holy offerings
Of rich sacrifice from men who dwell all around."
So spoke Telphusa, that fame in the land be her own
And not the Far-Darter's, and the Far-Darter's heart was persuaded.

Thereafter still farther you traveled, far-shooting Apollo,
Till you came to the city of arrogant Phlegyan men,
Those who are heedless of Zeus and dwell on the earth
In a beautiful glen close by the Cephissian lake.
Then, hastening on, you climbed toward the ridge and came quickly
To Crisa, under the snow-mantled peak of Parnassos,
High on a shoulder facing the west, where overhead
Hangs a cliff and beneath runs a wild, wooded hollow.
There the lord Phoebus Apollo determined to build
His lovely temple, and spoke a word and ordained it:
"Here I intend to build a most beautiful temple,
A shrine of oracular wisdom for men. Here they will always

Bring me as offering hecatombs full and unblemished—
As many as live in the fertile Peloponnesos,
All they who dwell in Europe, and those from the sea-washed isles
Who come seeking truth—and I will proclaim to them all
Infallible wisdom and counsel in my rich temple."

   Speaking thus, Phoebus Apollo laid down the foundations
Throughout, making his temple wide and exceedingly long.
Men dear to the undying gods, Trophonios and Agamedes,
Sons of Erginos, then fixed stone blocks upon the foundations,
And the numberless tribes of mankind, working in polished stone,
Finished the temple to be forever famous in song.

   Nearby was a fine-flowing spring, where the lord, son of Zeus,
Slew with his mighty bow a female dragon,
A well-fed, powerful monster, savage and bloody,
Who worked many evils on men who lived in that land—
Much evil to them, and much to their long-shanked flocks.
Once she received from golden-throned Hera to raise as her own
The cruel and terrible Typhon, a bane to mortals,
Whom Hera, angered by father Zeus, brought forth at the time
The son of Cronos gave birth from his head to glorious Athene.
Queenly Hera, enraged, spoke among the assembled immortals:

   "Hear me, all you gods and all goddesses too,
Learn how Zeus the cloud-gatherer begins now to do me dishonor
For the first time since he made me his trusted wife.
Now without me he has given birth to owl-eyed Athene,
Prominent among all the blessed immortals,
But the child I myself bore, Hephaistos, among all the gods
Was born a cripple, shriveled of foot, a shame
To me and a disgrace to heaven, and with my own hands
I picked him up and hurled him down into the broad sea.
But silvery-footed Thetis, the daughter of Nereus,
Welcomed him and with her sisters took care of the infant.
Would she had rendered some other service to the blessed immortals!
Devious wretch! What further outrage will you contrive?
How dared you by yourself to give birth to owl-eyed Athene!
Would not I have willingly borne you a child? I who at least
Am called your wife among the immortals who live in wide heaven?
Beware now lest I should devise some evil for you in return.
Truly I *will* find a way to give birth to a child of my own
Who will be outstanding among the undying gods.
But not by my act would I desecrate our sacred bed;

Nor will I come to your couch, but go my own way
Far from you among the other immortals."
   So speaking, Hera withdrew from the gods, her heart filled with anger.
Straightway, then, velvety-eyed lady Hera
Struck the earth with the flat of her hand, and called out in prayer:
   "Hear me now, earth and broad heaven above, and you Titans,
Gods dwelling around in great Tartaros under the ground,
You from whom men and gods have their being, all hear me now
And grant me a child without Zeus, lacking none of his strength,
But instead let him be as much stronger than Zeus
As far-seeing Zeus himself is stronger than Cronos."
Thus she cried out and flailed the ground with her thick hand.
Life-giving Earth was stirred, and Hera rejoiced
At the sight, and knew in her heart that her prayer would be answered.
From that time thereafter until a full year was completed,
Hera avoided the bed of Zeus wise in counsel,
Nor did she sit in the richly wrought chair by his side
As in former days, shrewdly pondering with him matters of state,
But, lingering in her temples of multitudinous prayer,
Soft-eyed lady Hera received with delight holy offerings from men.
When at last the months and the days were fulfilled as the seasons
     marched on
In the circling year, she bore one neither human nor godlike—
The cruel and terrible Typhon, a bane to mortals.
Forthwith, carrying evil to evil, ox-eyed lady Hera
Took him and gave him to the she-dragon, who gladly received him—
Typhon, who worked much evil among the illustrious tribes of mankind.
Whosoever encountered the dragon met also his doom,
For that day would carry him down to death, until lord Apollo
Who works from afar let fly at her his strong arrow.
The dragon, racked by unbearable pain, lay heavily
Gasping for breath and rolling about on the ground.
Then a hideous scream, past words to describe, split the air
As she thrashed back and forth in the wood, and she gave up her life,
Gushing it out blood-red, and Phoebus Apollo exulted:
   "Rot now, here on the man-nourishing earth!
No more will you live to be an abomination to mortals
Who eat of the fruit of the bountiful earth and will bring
To this place perfect hecatombs. Neither Typhoeus nor the Chimera
Of loathsome repute can ward off foul death from you now,
But here will black Earth and gleaming Hyperion cause you to rot."

So spoke Apollo in triumph, and darkness covered her eyes.
The sacred fire of Helios rotted her there on the spot
In the place now called Pytho,* and "Pythian" men dubbed the lord,
For there the searing power of Helios rotted the monster.
  And then Phoebus Apollo perceived in his heart
How the sweet-flowing spring, taking thought for her own, had
      deceived him,
And, angered, set out for Telphusa and quickly arrived.
He stood very near and spoke a word and addressed her:
  "Telphusa, did you intend to beguile my mind,
And keep for yourself this lovely place to pour out your sweet-
      flowing water?
Here shall my glory be also, and not yours alone!"
  So spoke lord Apollo, he who works from afar,
And with a shower of rocks pushed over upon her a crag,
Hiding her stream from sight. Then in a wooded grove
Close by the clear-running spring he erected an altar.
There all offer their vows to the lord as Apollo Telphusian,
Because he disfigured the stream of holy Telphusa.
  Then Phoebus Apollo considered well in his heart
Which of mankind he should bring in to serve him as priests
In his sacred temple precinct in rocky Pytho.
While turning his thoughts about in his mind, he espied
Out on the wine-dark sea a swift ship and within it
Men many and noble, Cretans from Minoan Knossos,
Those who offer sacrifice to the lord
And proclaim the decrees of gold-bladed Phoebus Apollo,
However he may respond in oracular utterance
Out of the laurel leaves up in the hollow under Parnassos.
They in the black ship, bent on business and matters of trade,
Were sailing to sandy Pylos and to the men born in Pylos
When Phoebus Apollo came forth to meet them, rushing
Upon the swift ship in the sea in the shape of a dolphin,
And lay on the deck, a great monster and frightful to see.
None of the Cretans pondered the happening so as to know,
But desired only to cast off the dolphin, who shook the black ship
Every which way, causing the very timbers to tremble,
And they all sat in the hollow black ship, silent and fearful.
Nor did they loosen the tackle or let down the sail

---

* Derived here as if from *putho* = "rot."

Of the dark-prowed vessel, but held to the course they had set
With thongs of oxhide at journey's beginning, and from behind
A sweeping south wind sped the swift ship on its way.
Past Malea they sailed, first, and along the Laconian coast
To the sea-girdled city of Tainaron, stronghold of Helios
Who brings joy to mortals, where graze forever the flocks,
Thick-fleeced, of lord Helios, there in a land of delight.
The sailors desired to beach their ship on the shore of that land
And, disembarking, to ponder the marvel and with their eyes
See whether the monster would tarry behind on the hollow ship
Or bound back again into the swell of the salt, fishy sea.
But the well-built ship responded not to the rudder
But, holding its course, sailed alongside the fertile Peloponnesos,
And with the aid of the wind lord Apollo who works from afar
Easily guided it straight on its way. Sailing its course,
The ship came to Arene and lovely Argyphea,
Thryon, the ford of the Alpheus, well-founded Aipy,
And sandy Pylos, the home of men born in Pylos.
Past Cruni and Chalcis it sailed, and skirted by Dyme,
Then past shining Elis, land where the Epeians rule.
As the ship made its way toward Pherae, glorying in the fair wind
Sent by Zeus, out from under the clouds there appeared
To the sailors the distant steep peak of Ithaca's mountain;
Dulichion, too, and Same, and wooded Zacynthos.
When they had sailed around the whole island of Pelops,
Heading toward Crisa, there came into view the boundless gulf
That cuts off the mass of the fertile Peloponnesos.
Then by the decree of Zeus came a strong wind from the west,
Cold and blustery, rushing upon them out of the sky,
That the ship with all speed might come to the end of its journey
Through the salt waves of the sea. So back again
Toward the east and the rising sun they sailed, and lord Apollo,
Son of Zeus, led the way. When they reached vine-clad Crisa,
Visible from afar, they put in to the harbor,
And the seafaring ship scraped to rest on the sands.

   Then out of the ship like a star at midday shot lord Apollo
Who works from afar, and sparks in profusion flashed from him
And the blaze reached to heaven. Then he entered his shrine,
Sinking from sight between precious tripods, and there
Kindled a flame that flared up and showed forth his arrows.
All Crisa was filled with its radiance, and the richly robed wives

And daughters of Crisa cried out at the bright burst of Phoebus,
For he threw great awe into all. Then bounding forth from his shrine,
He flew swift as thought back once more to the ship,
Seeming this time a vigorous man and strong,
In the flower of his youth, and his long hair lay along his broad shoulders.
And he spoke to the Cretans, addressing them with winged words:
　　"O strangers, who are you? From what land do you sail
Over the watery ways of the sea? Are you merchants,
Or do you rove aimlessly over the waves, like pirates
Who wander about risking their own lives and bringing evil to others?
Why thus do you loiter, cowering, and why do you not go ashore,
Disembarking, or take down the rigging of the black ship?
For such is the custom of seafaring men who venture for profit
Whenever they come to land from over the deep sea
In the black ship, sated with toil, and a longing
For sweet food assails them at once in their vitals."
　　So spoke Apollo, filling their hearts with courage,
And the leader among the Cretans spoke in reply:
"Stranger—yet you are like no one of mortal kind
In conformation or stature, but like the immortal gods—
Health to you and great joy, and may the gods grant you
Blessings. And now tell me truly that I may well know:
What place is this? What country? What people live here?
With a different journey in mind we were sailing on the great sea
Bound for Pylos from Crete, the land we claim as our birthplace.
Now we have come with our ship to this place all unwilling—
Another way, other paths—and we long to return to our home.
But one of the immortal gods led us hither against our will."
　　Then Apollo who works from afar, replying, addressed them:
"Strangers, you who before dwelt around well-wooded Knossos,
No more now will you return to your beloved city,
Each to his beautiful home and his cherished wife,
But here will you keep my rich temple honored by men without number.
I am the son of Zeus. Verily I am Apollo,
And I led you here over the boundless deep of the sea
Not intending you harm but that here you should keep
My rich temple and by all men be held in high honor.
You shall know the decrees of the gods, and by their will
Always, through all time to come, be deeply revered.
Come now, be persuaded, and quickly do as I tell you.
First lower the sails, loosing the thongs of ox leather,

Then drag the swift ship up onto the beach, and from it
Remove your goods and the gear of the well-balanced vessel;
Then build an altar upon the shore of the sea,
And kindle a fire, and sacrifice grains of white barley,
And pray, standing shoulder to shoulder around the altar.
As I first appeared to you in the form of a dolphin
Rushing upon the swift ship in the turbulent sea,
So pray to me as Delphinian,* and the altar itself
Shall be called Delphinian, all-overlooking forever.
Then make your meal alongside the swift black ship,
And pour a drink offering to the blessed gods of Olympus.
But when you have satisfied your desire for good food,
Come with me singing the paean in praise of the Healer—
Come to the place where you will keep my rich temple."

    So he spoke, and the Cretans heard and obeyed him.
First they loosened the thongs and let down the sails,
And lowered the mast by the forestays and set it to rest in the
      mast crutch,
Then disembarked in the surf at the edge of the sea.
They dragged the swift ship from the surf onto the mainland,
High up on the sands, and under it stretched long supports,
And erected an altar there on the shore of the sea,
And kindled a fire, and scattered upon it white barley
In sacrifice, and prayed, standing shoulder to shoulder
Around the altar, as lord Apollo had bidden.
Then they took their meal alongside the swift black ship,
And poured a drink offering to the blessed gods of Olympus.
But when they had put by their craving for drink and good food,
They set out with the son of Zeus, lord Apollo, who led them,
Holding a lyre in his hands and playing beautiful music
And stepping high and nimbly before them, and the Cretans, stamping
The earth in the dance, followed after. To Pytho they went,
Hymning the paean, like the chanters of Crete,
And those in whose hearts the heavenly Muse has instilled honeyed song.
Unwearied, on foot they ascended the ridge and soon reached
Parnassos and the lovely spot where they were destined to dwell,
Honored by men without number, and Apollo, leading them,
Showed them his most holy innermost shrine and the rich temple.

    Their spirit was stirred in their breasts and, voicing their questions,
The chief of the Cretans, confronting Apollo, addressed him:

---

  * *delphin* = "dolphin"

"O lord, if indeed you have led us hither, far away
From our loved ones and native land—for somehow this seems dear
    to your heart—
How are we now to live? We beg you to tell us.
Though pleasant, this place is not suited for vines, nor has it fair meadows
To let us live well that we may at the same time serve men."
    And, smiling upon them, Apollo, the son of Zeus, answered:
"Foolish men, suffering ones, you who wish in your heart
For sorrows and troublesome toil and desperate straits!
Easily will I tell you and plant the word in your minds.
Each of you holding a knife in his right hand could kill sheep
Forever, and as much as the glorious tribes of mankind
Bring to me here, all this will freely be yours.
But keep watch over my temple and welcome the tribes of mankind
That here assemble, and make known above all my purpose to mortals.
And you in your own hearts be righteous. If any through folly
Or heedlessness fails to obey me—some idle word it may be,
Or an arrogant deed, for such is the way of men who are mortal—
Then other men will be placed over you as your masters,
And you perforce will be under their yoke for all of your days.
All has been told you, and you guard it well in your hearts."
    And so farewell to you, son of Zeus and of Leto,
But I will remember you and another song too.

· 4 · To Hermes ·

SING, Muse, of Hermes, the son of Zeus and of Maia,
  Guardian over Cyllene and sheep-rich Arcadia,
  Luck-bringing messenger of the immortals, whom Maia,
  Shy, lovely-haired nymph, brought forth of her union in love
With Zeus. Shunning the company of the blessed immortals,
She lived in a shadowy cave, where Zeus son of Cronos
Came often by night to lie with the lovely-haired nymph
In the deep silent hours when sweet sleep possessed white-armed Hera,
Escaping thereby the observance of undying gods and of men.
But when the purpose of powerful Zeus was accomplished
And the tenth moon of Maia hung high in heaven,
She brought forth into the light, and his ruse was revealed.
The son she bore then was a versatile child, wily and wheedling,
A thief and a drover of cattle, a marshal of dreams,
By night a spy on watch at the gates, destined forthwith
To make manifest glorious deeds among the immortals.
Born in the morning, at midday he played on the lyre,
And at eventide stole the cows of far-shooting Apollo,
On the fourth day of the month—the day Maia bore him.
After he leapt from the immortal loins of his mother,
He tarried no longer to lie asleep in his holy cradle,
But rose up at once to go in search of the cows of Apollo.
He clambered over the sill of the high-vaulted cavern,
Where to his endless delight he discovered a tortoise—
Hermes it was who first made the tortoise a singer—
Coming upon it by chance at the gate of the courtyard
As, awkwardly mincing along on hesitant feet,
It browsed on the lush green grass in front of the dwelling.
Zeus' child, the luck-bringer, looked closely and laughed, and
    straightway spoke a word:
  "A most useful token for me already! Not I one to scorn it!
Hail, lovely creature, stamping the ground in the dance,
Comrade of the feast! Welcome indeed is your coming!
Where did you get that handsome bauble you wear, O tortoise,

You who live in the mountains—that patterned shell?
But let me carry you into the house. You will be useful
To me; I will show you no lack of honor, but first you must serve me.
Inside the house is better; out of doors there is danger.
Alive you will be a shield against baneful enchantment,
But if you should die, then would you sing with great beauty."
　　So Hermes spoke and, picking the creature up with both hands,
Went back into the house with his lovely new plaything.
There with a knife of gray iron he cut off the legs
And bored out the life of the mountain-bred tortoise.
As a swift thought courses through the heart of a man
Who writhes under close-crowding troubles, or as sparks flash
　　　from his eyes,
So at the same moment did glorious Hermes merge plan and deed.
He fixed at measured intervals cut stalks of reed
Through the clean-scooped shell of the tortoise and spanning the back,
And, by a stroke of wisdom, stretched oxhide over the hollow.
He added two horns to the sides yoked by a crossbar,
From which he stretched taut seven strings made of sheepgut.
When it was finished, he lifted the lovely toy on his arm
And tried each string in turn with the plectrum, and under his hand
A strange new sound rang out, and the god, trying his skill,
Sang along in sweet random snatches, as at festivals
Boys in the springtime of youth maliciously carol—
Singing of Zeus son of Cronos and Maia, beautifully sandaled,
And of their former intimate love and communion,
Recounting the tale of his own famous birth and begetting.
He honored as well the handmaids of the nymph and her glorious
　　　halls
And the tripods throughout her household and caldrons galore.
　　While yet Hermes sang, he yearned in his heart for new things.
He carried the hollow lyre to his holy wickerwork cradle
And there laid it down; then, craving the taste of flesh,
Forth from the sweet-scented chamber he sallied, and sprang to a
　　　lookout,
His mind turning over devices of deepest deception,
Deeds such as robbers arrange in the time of black night.
　　Helios was driving his chariot and horses from earth
Downward toward Ocean when Hermes arrived all in haste
In Pieria's shadowy mountains, there where the heavenly cattle
Of the blessed immortal gods had their stables and, sheltered,

Placidly grazed the lovely meadows unmown and fragrant.
The son of Maia, far-sighted slayer of Argos,
Cut out from the sacred herd fifty loud-bellowing beasts,
And drove them by random ways through the sandy places,
Turning their hoofprints aside; then he chanced on the crafty conceit
Of reversing their hoofs, so that their forefeet came after,
Their hind feet before, and he himself walked behind them.
Then on the sandy shore of the sea he wove wicker sandals—
Marvelous things they were, unthought of, unheard of—
Intermingling tamarisk branches and myrtlelike boughs.
He tied up in a bundle an armful of new-sprouted wood,
Leaves and all, and bound as light sandals securely under his feet
The bundles of boughs he gathered, the glorious slayer of Argos,
Preparing thus for his journey home from Pieria
As one hard-pressed prepares for a wearisome road.
    But an old man tending his flowering vineyard saw him
As he hurried down to the plain through grassy Onchestos.
The son of glorious Maia spoke first and addressed him:
    "Old fellow, you who among your vines dig with bent shoulders,
Rich in wine will you be when all these vines bear
If you heed me and remember well in your heart,
Seeing, not to have seen, and, having heard, to be mute.
Be silent except when some harm has been done to your own."
    So much he said, then drove on with his herd of strong cattle.
On through countless shadowy mountains and rushing ravines
And flowery plains did glorious Hermes drive them,
Until divine night, his dark ally, had for the greater part
Covered her course, and dawn that calls man to work was fast breaking,
And shining Selene, daughter of royal lord Pallas,
Son fathered by Megamedes, had newly ascended her watchtower.
Down then to the river Alpheus Hermes, stout son of Zeus,
Drove the broad-fronted cattle of Phoebus Apollo.
Unwearied, at length they came to the high-vaulted byre
And the watering troughs before the magnificent meadow.
When Hermes had seen the loud-lowing cattle well sated with fodder,
He rounded them up and herded them into their stable,
Still munching on lotus and galingale sprinkled with dew.
Then the god gathered wood in abundance, and sought after the
    technique of fire.
Grasping a branch of bright laurel, he peeled off the bark with his
    knife,

· · ·

Held close in the palm of his hand, and the hot blast burst forth.
Hermes thus first of all gave man fire and the kindling of fire.
Then he stacked thick in a pit dug in the ground
Dry, seasoned logs without stint, and the flame grew and brightened,
Sending far distant the blaze of hot-burning fire.

While the power of glorious Hephaistos was feeding the flame,
Hermes, endowed with great strength, dragged out of the stable
To a spot near the fire two lowing, crumple-horned beasts,
And threw them, both panting, down on their backs on the ground,
And, rolling them over, forced back their heads and bored out their
　　lives.
Deed he added to deed. He cut up the meat rich with fat,
And, piercing the morsels with wooden spits, roasted the flesh,
Along with the chine highly honored and the black blood
Confined in the entrails, and these he laid on the ground.
The hides he stretched on a steep slab of rough unhewn rock,
And so they remain even now, long ages since they were placed there—
Ages long past these events, and forever unchanging.
Next, joyous-hearted, Hermes hauled the rich meat
To a smooth, flat stone and divided it into twelve portions,
Sharing it out by lot, and conferring to each his due measure of
　　honor.
Then, tempted, glorious Hermes yearned for a taste of the meat
Unreserved to the gods, for the pleasant odor of roasting
Distressed even him, an immortal, but his strong heart was steadfast;
No morsel slid down his holy throat however great was his yearning.
Instead, he carried inside the high-vaulted byre
The fat and a mound of roast flesh and, hoisting them quickly aloft,
There laid them up in remembrance of his youthful theft.
Then, gathering dry sticks together, he covered his traces,
Destroying all the feet and the thickly curled heads
Of the two slain beasts in the hot blaze of the fire.

When all his work at last was completed, the god
Tossed his tamarisk sandals deep into the eddying Alpheus
And put out the embers and strewed over with sand the black ashes.
All through the night he labored, while the lovely light of Selene
　　shone down,
Then at dawn scurried back to the shining peaks of Cyllene;
Nor did anyone either of blessed gods or of mortals
Encounter him on the long journey, or any dog bark.
Then luck-bringing Hermes, begotten by Zeus, turning sideways,
Made his way into the hall of his home through the keyhole

Like a breeze in autumn, or incorporeal mist.
He slipped straight through the cave to the rich inner chamber,
His silent feet making no sound as they might on the ground.
Climbing quickly back into his wickerwork cradle, glorious Hermes
Drew around him his swaddling wraps, enfolding his shoulders,
Seeming an infant newborn and helpless, and, as he lay,
Played with his hands at the coverings over his knees
While under his left arm he sheltered his lovely tortoise.
But the god eluded not the eye of the goddess his mother.
    "Where do you come sneaking home from, you rascal," she said,
        "at this time of night,
You of consummate wiles, clad in shamelessness? Very soon now,
I foresee, you will quickly be helplessly bound with strong bands
Close round the ribs by the hand of Leto's Apollo,
And carried bodily out the front door—not playing your tricks
Down in the glens and the hollows robbing betweentimes.
Back with you again where you came from! Your father begot you
To be a great nuisance to mortal men and the undying gods!"
    Hermes then answered her, craftily choosing his words:
"Mother mine, why do you welcome me with these threats and
        forebodings,
Like an innocent child who knows very little of evil,
A baby who shrinks with fright when his mother reproves him?
Me, I shall hit upon some clever scheme—what may be best—
And so provide food for you and for me for all time.
Not for us two, alone among the undying gods
Unfeed by gifts and unprayed to, patiently here to abide as you bid.
Better to spend all our days among the immortals,
Rich and prosperous, owning productive acres of cornland,
Than to sit at home in a drafty cave. As to honor,
I too will enter into the rites Apollo enjoys.
But if my father withholds the gift, then indeed I will try—
And doubt not that I can—to become the prince among robbers.
And if the son of all-glorious Leto searches me out,
Something else even worse, I predict, will befall him,
For I will go and break into his great house at Pytho
And plunder it of its hoard of beautiful tripods and caldrons
And gold and flashing iron in abundance and many fine garments.
You shall see all of it, mother, if you desire."
    So with such words they spoke one to another, Hermes,
The son of Zeus of the aegis, and heavenly Maia.

Dawn, early-born, who brings light to mortals, was rising
Out of deep-flowing Ocean when Phoebus Apollo
Came, on his way, to Onchestos, the lovely green grove
Consecrate to Poseidon, loud-roaring Upholder of Earth.
There the son of all-glorious Leto found the old man
Grazing his beast by the path through the hedge of his courtyard,
And Apollo, halting his strides, spoke first and addressed him:
    "Old man, you who gather the brambles of grassy Onchestos,
I come to this place from Pieria seeking my cattle,
All of the creatures cows, all having long crumpled horns,
Part of my herd—the bull, blue-black, grazed alone,
Away from the others. And fierce-eyed dogs followed after the herd—
Four, like-minded as men. But the dogs and the bull
Were all left behind—a marvelous thing to have happened.
The cows strayed off at the time the sun was just setting,
Away from the soft, grassy meadow, away from the succulent pasture.
Tell me, old man born long ago, if by chance you have seen
Some man passing by on the road driving my cattle."
    The old man, replying, then spoke to him in these words:
"Dear friend, a difficult task to say all I have seen
With my eyes. For many wayfarers pass back and forth
On this road, some bent on evil, others on good.
Hard would it be to know all about every one.
But all day until sundown I was here in my vineyard
Digging about, tending my fruitful vines.
And I seemed, sir, to see—but I cannot certainly say—
A young child, some boy, who herded before him horned cattle,
An infant who carried a staff and roamed from one side to another,
But, oddly, he drove the cows backwards, their heads facing toward
    him."
    So spoke the old man, and Apollo, hearing his words,
The more quickly went on his way. Not long thereafter
He glimpsed a wide-winged bird of omen, and straightway he knew
That the culprit he sought was the child born of Zeus son of Cronos.
So, concealed by a purple cloud around his broad shoulders,
The son of Zeus, lord Apollo, rushed impetuously on
To most holy Pylos in search of his sway-gaited cattle.
Then he saw tracks, and Apollo, Far-Darter, cried out:
    "By my bow! What I see with my eyes is truly a wonder!
These tracks are surely the hoofprints of fine long-horned cattle,
But back they turn toward the asphodel meadow; these others—

Such prints are not those of man nor yet those of woman,
Nor of gray wolves, neither of bears, nor of lions,
Nor do I think they are those of a shaggy-necked centaur,
This creature that takes such enormous strides on swift feet.
Fearsome are these on this side of the path, more fearsome those
    on the other!"

    So saying, the son of Zeus, lord Apollo, sped on
And came to the forest-clad peak of Cyllene, to the shadowy cavern
Cut deep in the rock where Maia, the immortal nymph,
Had brought forth to light the child of Zeus son of Cronos.
A delicate fragrance hung over the hallowed mountain,
And flocks of long-shanked sheep grazed on the grass.
Far-shooting Apollo himself then stepped swiftly over
The threshold of stone and entered the cave dark with shadows.

    Now Hermes, the son of Zeus and of Maia, observing
The wrath of Apollo, Far-Darter, concerning his cattle,
Nestled deep into his sweet-smelling swaddling garments.
As wood ash envelops the glowing embers of tree trunks,
So Hermes buried himself when he saw the Far-Worker.
He made of himself a small bundle, drawing up arms
And legs toward his head, as though, fresh from his bath,
He was drifting into sweet slumber. In truth, wide awake
And watchful he lay, and held his lyre under his armpit.
But the son of Zeus and of Leto failed not to perceive
Both the beautiful nymph of the mountains and her dear son,
That little child, lying there wrapped in deceit.
Intently, Apollo looked round the cavernous dwelling,
Carefully peering into each dusky corner;
Then with a shiny key he unlocked three cupboards,
And found them full of nectar and lovely ambrosia.
Much gold and silver lay also within them, and many
Crimson and silvery robes of the nymph, such things
As are kept in the sacred homes of the blessed immortals.
When he had searched every nook of the cavernous dwelling,
The son of Leto turned and accosted glorious Hermes:

    "Boy, you who lie there in your wickerwork cradle,
Tell me at once what you have done with my cows,
Or we two shall fall out in a way neither seemly nor proper.
For I will take you and hurl you down into gloomy Tartaros,
Doomed to darkness, and helpless; nor shall your mother
Or father free and restore you to daylight, but under the earth

You shall wander forever, the leader among little people."

Hermes then answered Apollo, craftily choosing his words:
"Son of Leto, what are all these harsh things that you say?
Have you come here seeking cows that graze in the meadows?
I have not seen them or heard of them, nor have I had
Word from another about them. I could disclose
Nothing about them, even to win a reward.
I am not a strong man, not like a rustler of cattle.
Not mine is this deed; I have quite other concerns.
Sleep do I care for more, and the milk of my mother,
To have swaddling clothes over my shoulders, and be given warm
    baths.
Let no one hear from what matter this quarrel arose,
For it would be a great wonder among the immortals
That a child newly born, a mere babe, should pass through the
    front door
Driving before him cows of the field. What nonsense you speak!
I was born yesterday. Soft are my feet and the ground beneath rough.
But, if you wish, I will swear a great oath by the head of my father:
Neither, I vow, am I myself guilty of what you accuse me,
Nor have I seen any other thief stealing your cows—
Whatever cows may be; I know them only by rumor."

So Hermes spoke, his shrewd eyes sparkling and twinkling,
And he wiggled his eyebrows, glancing hither and yonder,
And absent-mindedly whistled, as if hearing an idle tale.

Apollo who works from afar, softly laughing, replied:
"You little imp, you deceiver, wily of mind,
To hear you talk, I could well believe that last night
You broke into many a well-furnished house, and left more than
One poor wretch only the floor to sit on,
While you soundlessly went through the rooms, stripping them bare.
And many a shepherd dwelling alone in the fields
Will you harass in the mountain glens when you hunger for meat
And come upon herds of cattle and wool-bearing sheep.
But come, if you would not that this sleep now be your last,
Get down out of your cradle, companion of black night,
For now and hereafter this honor you hold among the immortals:
You shall for all time be known as the prince among robbers."

So spoke Phoebus Apollo, and picked up the child
And carried him off. But the mighty slayer of Argos,
Musing as he was borne away in the arms of Apollo,

Sent forth an omen—a rude, importunate herald—
Exploding a belch from his belly, and followed that blast with a sneeze
Apollo, hearing him, let Hermes fall from his arms to the ground
And, though longing to be on his way, sat down before him
And spoke a few words, gently gibing at Hermes:

"Have no fear, little baby enveloped in swaddling clothes,
Son of Zeus and of Maia. I will yet find
My herd of strong cows, and by these very omens,
And you shall go before and show me the way."

So he spoke, and Cyllenian Hermes quickly jumped to his feet,
And with both hands readjusted the swaddling wraps
Wound round his shoulders, pushing them up to his ears.
Then he turned and spoke a word to Apollo:

"Where do you carry me, Far-Worker, hottest-tempered of all gods?
Is it because of your cows that you rave so and persecute me?
Oh, I would that the race of cows would perish, believe me!
I did not steal your cows or see any other who did—
Whatever cows may be; I know them only by rumor.
But dispense and receive right before Zeus son of Cronos."

So over each separate term they disputed and wrangled,
Hermes the shepherd and Leto's beautiful son,
And each one held fast. But Apollo, with unerring voice

. . .

Not without ground did he clash with glorious Hermes
Over his cows, but the wily Cyllenian tried
With ruses and tricks and flattering words to deceive
The lord of the silver bow. Yet, finding the other
Fertile in tricks of his own, he of many devices,
Leading, rapidly trotted ahead through the sand,
And the son of Zeus and of Leto followed behind.
Soon they came to the heights of sweet-smelling Olympus,
The surpassingly beautiful children of Zeus son of Cronos,
And to their father, for there lay the scales of justice for both.
A convocation was being assembled on snow-capped Olympus,
And the undying gods gathered together just after gold-enthroned
   dawn.

Hermes and lord Apollo, god of the silver bow,
Stood side by side seeking judgment before the knees of their father.
Then high-thundering Zeus spoke a word to his son shining in beauty:

"Phoebus, where do you come from, driving this winsome captive,
This child newly born, having the look of a herald?

Serious business, this, that you bring to the council of gods!"
    Lord Apollo who works from afar replied in return:
"Father, you will soon hear an incredible tale,
Though you taunt me and hold that I alone care for plunder.
I found a child—this very one—a burglar and thief,
In the hills of Cyllene after traveling far through the land.
Another such mocker have I never seen among gods,
Or men, for that matter, as many swindlers on earth as there are.
He stole my cows from their meadow and drove them away
In the dusk of evening along the shore of the loud-roaring sea,
Making directly for Pylos. The tracks behind him were double,
The tracks of a monster, tracks to give rise to wonder,
The spoor of an ingenious devil. As for the cows,
The black dust proclaimed that their footsteps led toward the
        asphodel meadow.
He himself wandered aside from the path, and—I cannot explain it—
Traversed the sandy places on neither his feet nor his hands.
By some other means he knew he pursued his journey—
Some magic—as if one might walk on slender young oak trees.
So long as he drove the cows through the sandy places,
The tracks they left in the dust were all very clear,
But when he had put behind him the long stretch of sand,
The hoofprints of cows and his own tracks faded away
And soon became indiscernible on the hard ground.
A man, a mortal, noticed him heading for Pylos
Driving before him the herd of broad-fronted cattle.
When he had quietly shut them in for the night,
He returned to his home, playing with fire here and there on the way,
Then silently as black night he crept into his cradle
Down in the darkness of the dim cave—not even
An eagle on watch would have spotted him with his sharp eyes.
The child, when I charged him, rubbed his eyes hard, inventing
        fresh schemes,
Then at once, careless of consequence, uttered a word:
'I have not seen them or heard of them, nor have I had
Word from another about them. I could disclose
Nothing about them, even to win a reward.'"
    When he had spoken, Phoebus Apollo sat down.
Hermes then, standing opposite, made his defense,
Pointing at Zeus son of Cronos, king of all gods.
    "Zeus, father, to you will I tell the absolute truth,

For I am unfailingly honest and do not know how to lie.
He came to our cave in search of his sway-gaited cows
Early this morning, just as the sun was new-rising.
None of the blessed gods had he brought along with him—
No observer or witness—but with great show of force
Demanded of me to make known what I had done with his cows,
And strongly threatened to hurl me down into broad Tartaros.
He bears the delicate bloom of joyful young manhood,
While I, a baby, was born yesterday—he too knows this.
I am not a strong man, not like a drover of cattle.
Believe me, for you profess to be my father too.
I did not drive his cows home—so may I prosper!—
Nor did I cross over the threshold. This that I speak is the truth.
Helios and the other gods I hold in high reverence,
You do I love, and I care too for him. You yourself know
That I am not guilty, but I will swear a great oath—
Not by these well-adorned porticoes of the immortals!
Sometime, somehow, strong as he is, I will pay Phoebus back
For his ruthless grilling. But you, father, come to the aid of the younger."
  So spoke Cyllenian Hermes, the slayer of Argos,
Rapidly blinking his eyes, his swaddling wraps,
Undiscarded, draped carelessly over his arm.
Zeus laughed aloud seeing his child wise in evil
Denying well and with cunning all knowledge concerning the cattle.
He bade them both then, with their minds in agreement, set out
And seek after the cows, with Hermes the guide leading the way
And pointing out to Apollo, without thought of mischief,
The place where he had concealed the herd of fine cattle.
And Zeus son of Cronos nodded, confirming his word.
Hermes, brilliant in splendor, obeyed, for the will
And purpose of Zeus, aegis-bearer, quickly prevailed.
  Then the two surpassingly beautiful children of Zeus
Hastened to sandy Pylos, and came to the ford of the Alpheus
And the fields and the high-vaulted byre where by night the cattle
    were sheltered.
Hermes then, going inside the stony cave of the byre,
Drove out into the light the herd of fine cattle.
But the son of Leto, glancing around, saw the hides
Stretched on a towering rock, and sharply addressed glorious Hermes:
  "How were you able, you devious-minded child,
To slaughter two cows, being so very newborn and helpless?

I myself shudder to think of the strength to be yours
Hereafter. There is no need for you to grow tall,
Little Cyllenian, son of heavenly Maia."
　So spoke Apollo, and twisted around in his hands
Tough willow shoots with which to fashion strong fetters,
Desiring to bind glorious Hermes. But bonds would not hold him,
And the willow withes fell off at a distance around him
And took root in the earth underfoot and began to grow
There on the spot, shooting up quickly and twining around
One another and all the cattle that graze in the meadows,
By the will of Hermes of dissembling mind, while Apollo
Looked on in amazement. Then the strong slayer of Argos
Covertly scanned the ground, his eyes sparkling with fire,

. . .

Seeking to find a hollow to hide in, but Hermes,
As he had designed, easily soothed the Far-Darter,
Son of most glorious Leto, obdurate though he was.
Taking his lyre upon his left arm, he tried out
Each string in turn with the plectrum, and under his hand
The lyre resounded uncannily. Phoebus Apollo
Laughed aloud with delight. The lovely sound
Of heavenly music went straight through his heart, and sweet longing
Possessed him as he listened, enraptured. As he played on,
Enticingly stroking his lyre, the young son of Maia,
Gaining assurance, sidled up to the left
Of Phoebus Apollo, and soon, still calling forth
Clear strains from the lyre, he burst into song—and lovely his voice—
Telling of how the immortal gods and black earth
First came to be, and how each was allotted his portion.
Mnemosyne, mother of Muses, first of the gods
He honored with song, for to her Maia's son was apportioned by lot.
Hermes, the son brilliant in splendor of Zeus,
Hymned the undying gods according to age,
And told the tale of how each one was born, relating
All things in order, to the sweet strains of the lyre on his arm.
The anguish of helpless desire laid hold on the heart of Apollo,
And he cried out to Hermes, addressing him with winged words:
　"Killer of cows, prankster, industrious child,
Comrade of the feast, your invention is worth fifty cows!
I think we shall very soon peacefully settle our quarrel.
Now come, tell me this, versatile son of Maia:

Has this wondrous object been yours since your birth, or did one
Of the immortal gods or someone of mortal mankind
Give you this royal gift and coach you in heavenly song?
So amazing is this new sound that I hear
That no man, I swear, can ever have heard it before,
Nor any of the immortals who have their homes on Olympus
Save you, you robber, son of Zeus and of Maia.
What art can this be? What music for hearts bent with sorrow?
What path of life? For here in truth are combined
Three pleasures to choose from—merriment, love, and sweet slumber.
I, though attendant upon the Olympian Muses,
Who take careful thought for the dance and the bright strains of song,
The swelling chant and the sweet shrilling of pipes,
Never before have I cared so much in my heart
For other displays of skill by festive young men.
Son of Zeus, I am astonished, so lovely your playing!
And now, since although indeed you are little you have such
    remarkable talent,
Sit down here, my friend, and heed the voice of your elders.
Now fame and glory will be yours among the immortals,
For both you yourself and your mother—I truly proclaim it.
I swear by this cornelwood shaft I will make you a leader
Renowned and blessed among the immortals and give you rich gifts,
And to the end of the world I will never deceive you."
    Hermes then answered him, craftily choosing his words:
"You question me closely, Far-Worker, but not out of envy
Would I deny you the means of learning my art.
This very day you shall know it. Toward you would I always be
Kindly in words and intending. But you in your heart, son of Zeus,
Well know all things, for you sit foremost among the immortals,
Both brave and strong, and Zeus wise in counsel loves you
And with all justice has granted you glorious favors.
From the divine voice of Zeus they say you have learned
The honors due to the gods, Far-Worker, and know
By oracular power all that Zeus has decreed.
I have heard too that you are exceedingly rich;
It is for you to choose to learn whatever delights you.
But since now your heart is set on playing the lyre,
Receive it from me, and sing and play and be happy,
And you, my friend, on me bestow future glory.
Sing well as you hold in your hands the clear-voiced companion,

For you are skilled in beautiful speech according to order.
Then, carefree, carry joy to the bounteous feast,
The lovely choral dance, and the brilliant carousal
By night and day. For whoever with wisdom and skill
Inquires of it, him will it teach, in a voice loud and clear,
All manner of things agreeable to the mind,
Being played lightly with delicate, intimate touches,
For it loathes painful toil. But he who, witless to start with, asks roughly,
Him will it answer with wavering notes and uncertain noises.
But it is for you to choose to learn whatever delights you.
Son radiant in splendor of Zeus, I will give you this lyre,
And I in turn, Far-Worker, will graze down the pastures
Of mountain and horse-feeding plain with cattle that dwell in the
  meadows.
Then cows shall be covered by bulls and bring forth in abundance
Calves, both heifers and bull calves. So there is no reason for you,
Shrewd at a trade as you are, to fly into a rage."

So speaking, he held out the lyre, and Phoebus Apollo received it,
And of his own will gave into the hand of Hermes
The shining scourge, and ordained him herder of cattle,
And the son of Maia, rejoicing, received it. Then Apollo,
Lord who works from afar, Leto's illustrious son,
Took the lyre upon his left arm and tried out with the plectrum
Each string in turn, and under his deft touch the strains
Of unearthly music rang out, while the god sang along.

Then together they turned the cows back toward the sacred meadow,
And themselves, the surpassingly beautiful children of Zeus,
Hastened once more to snowy Olympus, exultant
Over the lyre. Zeus wise in counsel was glad
And brought his sons together in friendship. Hermes,
From that moment when, having taught Apollo the art,
He gave the longed-for lyre as a token into his hands
And the Far-Darter took it upon his left arm and played—
Hermes from that time forever loved Leto's son,
And so even now. Then from his vast store of knowledge
Hermes devised a new art and, joining cut reeds,
Fashioned the syrinx, whose shrill sound is heard from afar.

Then Apollo, the son of Leto, spoke words to Hermes:
"I am afraid, son of Maia, guide, wily of mind,
Lest you should steal from me the lyre and my bent bow together,
For from Zeus you hold the honor of bringing to men

Throughout the all-nourishing earth business of barter.
But if you dare swear to me the great oath of the gods,
Either by nodding your head or by the strong waters of Styx,
You would do all I could ask for to ease and win over my heart."

The son of Maia then, nodding his head, solemnly vowed
Never to steal the Far-Darter's many possessions
And never to venture near his thickly built house, and Apollo,
Son of Leto, nodded in turn, vowing friendship and love
And swearing to hold dearer than Hermes no other
Among the immortals—neither god nor man born of Zeus.
And father Zeus sent out an eagle, confirming the oath.
Then Apollo furthermore swore: "You only, Hermes,
Among the immortal gods and all others besides
Will I adopt as a symbol of my heart's trust and esteem.
I will give you, moreover, a beautiful wand of blessing and riches,
Wrought of gold, triply entwined, to protect you, unharmed,
And bring to conclusion all contests of words and of deeds
Of the good that I claim to know from Zeus' divine voice.
But the art of prophecy, friend, god-cherished child,
About which you ask—it is not ordained that you learn it,
Or any other immortal; the mind of Zeus alone knows it.
I bound myself by a pledge, nodding, and swore a strong oath
That no one apart from me of the gods everlasting
Should ever share the wise-minded counsel of Zeus.
So do not press me, gold-wanded brother, to make clear his will
And reveal the decrees and intentions of far-seeing Zeus.
As for mankind, one man will I harm and another man benefit,
Greatly perplexing the tribes of unenviable men.
He who comes to my shrine, guided there by the cries
And flight of birds of sure omen, will reap a rich harvest
From my oracular voice, and I will not deceive him.
But he who, foolishly trusting in idly twittering birds,
Desires to inquire through my oracle into things beyond knowing
And to understand more than the gods everlasting—that man
I say travels the road without profit, though his gifts I would take.

"And this too I will tell you, son of all-glorious Maia
And of Zeus, aegis-bearer, of gods the spirit of luck.
Certain holy ones are there, three of them, sisters and virgins,
Adorned with swift wings, on whose heads has been sprinkled white
      barley,
Who live in a dwelling under a ledge of Parnassos.

Teachers of prophecy are they apart from me—
That art I studied while yet a boy tending cattle,
And my father at that time cared not at all.
From their mountain home they flit from one place to another,
Feeding on honeycombs, and they bring all things to fulfillment.
When they are inspired by eating pale golden honey,
Graciously then are they willing to utter the truth,
But if deprived of the sweet food of the gods,
They speak false words and swarm in confusion around one another.
These, then, I give you. Inquire sincerely of them
And be content in your heart. If you should so teach some mortal,
Often, if he is lucky, will he hear your response.
Take these, son of Maia, and watch over crumple-horned cattle
That graze in the meadows, and horses, and mules long-enduring."
    So spoke Apollo, and out of high heaven the father,
Zeus himself, brought to fulfillment the words of his son.
Zeus commanded besides that glorious Hermes rule over
All birds of omen and fiery-eyed lions and boars with white tusks,
And dogs and flocks, as many as broad earth feeds—
Over all beasts that move on the land—and moreover appointed
Hermes his son to serve as sole courier to Hades,
Who, though receiving no gifts, will himself give no unworthy prize.
    Thus lord Apollo showed love for the young son of Maia
With all these affectionate tokens, and Zeus son of Cronos
Besides showered favor upon him. Consorting with all gods and mortals,
Seldom he helps them, but everlastingly cozens
The tribes of mortal mankind throughout the dark night.
    And so farewell to you, son of Zeus and of Maia;
Yet I will remember you and another song too.

· 5 · To Aphrodite ·

MUSE, speak to me of the deeds of the Cyprian,
Aphrodite the golden, who stirs up sweet longing
In gods and subdues the tribes of mortal mankind
And birds that fly in the air and all wild beasts
Of the many kinds the dry land supports and the sea.
For all are concerned with the deeds of bright-crowned Cytherea.
    But three are the hearts she can neither sway nor beguile:
Gray-eyed Athene, daughter of Zeus, aegis-bearer,
Takes no delight in the deeds of Aphrodite the golden;
Pleasure for her lies in war and the grim work of Ares,
In fighting and battles and fostering glorious handcrafts.
She first taught the builders among men who live on the earth
How to fashion war chariots and cars inlaid with bronze,
And taught smooth-skinned palace maidens at work in their quarters
To weave with bright strands, implanting the art in each mind.
Nor ever has Aphrodite, lover of smiles,
Brought Artemis of the hunting cry and arrow of gold
Under her yoke of love, for the bow and arrow
Are her delight, and slaying wild beasts in the mountains,
And the sound of the lyre and dancing and joyful cries
And shadowy groves and the cities of righteous men.
Nor do the deeds of Aphrodite charm Hestia,
Modest and maidenly, first-born of Cronos crooked of counsel,
But by the devising of Zeus, aegis-bearer, also his youngest,
The great lady wooed by Poseidon and Phoebus Apollo.
But she, reluctant to marry, steadfastly refused them,
And swore a great oath, still faithfully being fulfilled,
Laying her hand on the head of the father, Zeus, aegis-bearer,
To remain a virgin for all of her days. And to her,
Bright among goddesses, Zeus gave high honor instead of marriage,
And she sits in the heart of the household receiving choice offerings.
In all the temples sacred to gods she is honored,
And by all mortals venerated above other gods.
    Their hearts Aphrodite can neither sway nor beguile.

But of others no one ever escapes Aphrodite,
Either of blessed gods or of mortal mankind.
Even Zeus who delights in loud thunder she leads into folly—
He who is greatest and has for his share the greatest of honors—
Even that wise heart she deceives at her pleasure
And lightly mates him with women of mortal mankind,
All unknown to Hera, his sister and wife,
Goddess surpassing by far in beauty the other immortals.
Cronos crooked of counsel begot her, all-glorious Hera,
On Rhea, her mother, and Zeus, whose wisdom forever endures,
Made her his cherished wife, chaste and devoted.

But into the heart of Aphrodite herself
Zeus cast sweet longing to lie in love with a man,
That not even she should escape the marriage bed of a mortal,
Lest at some time Aphrodite, lover of smiles,
Laughing sweetly in triumph, should boast that among all the gods
She had joined gods together with women of mortal mankind,
Who bore mortal sons to immortals, and mated with goddesses men.

So for Anchises Zeus aroused in her heart sweet desire,
A man godlike in form who was then tending cattle
Among the high-ranging hills of Ida abounding in fountains.
Aphrodite, lover of smiles, looked on him and loved him,
And desire and desperate longing laid hold on her heart.
She hastened to Cyprus and entered her sweet-smelling temple
In Paphos, where lay her sacred precinct and altar,
And shut behind her the gleaming doors of the shrine.
There the Graces bathed and anointed her, smoothing on
Ambrosial unguents such as perfume the gods everlasting—
Divinely fragrant oils of the goddess's own.
Then Aphrodite, lover of smiles, clothed in all her fine raiment,
Gold-adorned, flew to Troy, forsaking sweet-scented Cyprus.
Swiftly, high among clouds, she followed her way,
And came to many-springed Ida, mother of beasts,
Making straight for the farmstead over the mountain.
Gray wolves, fawning upon her, went with her; fierce lions, too,
And bears, and quick leopards, their hunger for roe deer ever unsated.
Aphrodite rejoiced in her soul at the sight,
And into the heart of each beast cast love and desire,
And all, two by two, lay down together among the dim shadows.

The goddess arrived at the well-built cabins and found him
Alone at the farmstead, left behind by his comrades,

The hero Anchises, in beauty like to the gods.
All the rest were away tending cattle in grassy meadows,
But Anchises, left by the others alone at the farmstead,
Strolled up and down calling forth thrilling sounds from his lyre.
Aphrodite, the daughter of Zeus, stood before him,
Seeming in height and appearance a maiden untouched,
Lest he be frightened by seeing her plain with his eyes.
Anchises beheld her in wonder, bemused and amazed
By her stately beauty and size and costly apparel,
For the robe she wore, fastened with glittering flower-shaped brooches,
Shone with a brilliance that dimmed the bright light of fire;
Her ears were adorned with bent earrings, and the beautiful necklaces
Circling her delicate throat were fashioned of gold richly wrought
And shimmered like moonlight around her soft breasts—a wonder to see.
   Love laid hold on Anchises, and to her he spoke:
"Welcome, queen, whoever of the blessed you are who come to
      this house—
Artemis, Leto, or Aphrodite the golden,
Themis highborn, or even gray-eyed Athene.
Or are you one of the lovely Graces who come here,
Companions to all the gods and ranked as immortal?
Or one of the nymphs who haunt the delectable groves,
Or of the nymphs who dwell on this beautiful mountain
And in the deep springs of rivers and in grassy meadows?
I will build you an altar high on the peak of the mountain
In view of the country around, and in all seasons bring you rich offerings.
And be well disposed yourself toward me in your heart.
Grant that I be a man high in honor among the Trojans,
The father hereafter of vigorous children, and for myself
Grant that I live long and well, seeing the light of the sun,
Happy among my people, and prosperous, up to the threshold of age."
   The daughter of Zeus, Aphrodite, then answered him, saying:
"Noble Anchises, most glorious of men born on earth,
I am no goddess. Why do you think me immortal?
Certainly I am a mortal, and a woman the mother who bore me.
My father is Otreus, a name of renown—no doubt you have heard it.
He rules over all of strongly fortified Phrygia.
Your tongue I know as well as my own, for in our palace
A Trojan nurse raised me, who had full charge from the time
I was a small child, receiving me from my dear mother.
So your language I know quite as well as my own.

Now the gold-wanded slayer of Argos has carried me off
From the choral dance of Artemis of the clear hunting cry
And arrow of gold. A crowd of us—nymphs and maidens
Courted by cattle-rich suitors—stepped to the beat,
And as we danced countless throngs circled round.
From them he snatched me away, the gold-wanded slayer of Argos,
And led me far over many tilled fields of mortal mankind
And lands unallotted and acres untouched by the plow
Where wild beasts that feed on raw flesh roam in the shadowy hollows,
Till I thought nevermore to touch with my feet the life-giving earth.
To the marriage bed of Anchises he told me he led me,
To be your lawful wife and to bear you strong children.
He told me and pointed you out and then went away,
The mighty slayer of Argos, back to the tribes of immortals.
And so I come to you led by unyielding necessity.
I entreat you before Zeus and your own noble parents—
For surely not baseborn are they who gave such a son life—
Lead me, a virgin untried in love, to your home
And show me to your father and careful-eyed mother
And to your brothers born of the same blood as you.
No unworthy daughter-in-law will I be, but most seemly.
And send off with all speed word to the swift-riding Phrygians
That my father may know and my mother, anxious indeed.
They will send you gold in abundance and fine woven garments;
Their many and glorious gifts receive as my dowry.
Do this, and make ready the feast for the lovely marriage
Honorable to men and the immortal gods."
    So speaking, Aphrodite cast into his heart sweet desire.
Love laid hold on Anchises, and he spoke from his heart:
    "If you are mortal in truth, and a woman the mother who bore you,
And Otreus of famous name is your father, as you declare,
And you come here by the grace of immortal Hermes the Guide
And for all time to come you will be known as my wife,
Then no one of the gods or of mortal mankind
Shall stay me from lying with you this moment in love—
Not even if the Far-Shooter, Apollo himself,
Should let fly from his silver bow his arrows of anguish.
Then would I willingly, woman like to the goddesses,
Make my way from your bed down into the house of Hades."
    So speaking, he took her hand, and the lover of smiles, Aphrodite,
Turning aside her face, her beautiful eyes cast down,

Hesitant, followed him to the comfortable bed
Earlier spread for the hero's repose with soft coverings,
Over them thrown the skins of bears and loud-roaring lions
Slain by Anchises himself in the towering mountains.
When they had climbed up onto the well-structured bed,
Anchises removed first of all her shining adornments—
Her necklaces, flower-shaped brooches, and helical earrings;
Then he loosened her girdle and stripped off her glittering gown
And laid it upon a settle studded with silver.
Thus, by the will of the gods and the dictates of fate,
He, a mortal, all unaware, lay with an immortal goddess.

But at the time when herdsmen drive back to the fold
From the flowery pastures their cattle and sturdy-shanked sheep,
Aphrodite poured over Anchises sweet dreamless slumber
And clothed herself in her beautiful raiment. At last,
Fully dressed, the queen among goddesses stood by the bed;
Her head reached to the well-hewn crossbeams, and from her cheeks
Immortal beauty shone forth—that of bright-crowned Cytherea.
She roused Anchises from slumber, calling his name, and addressed him:

"Wake up, son of Dardanos! Why do you spend the whole night
Sleeping so soundly? Consider now whether I seem
The same as before, when first your eyes fell upon me."

So spoke Aphrodite. Anchises, promptly awaking, heard and
obeyed her.
But when he beheld Aphrodite's throat and her beautiful eyes,
He shuddered with fear and, averting his gaze, turned aside
And hid his own noble face in the folds of his cloak
And addressed Aphrodite with winged words of entreaty:

"The very first moment my eyes looked upon you,
I knew, goddess, you were divine, but you spoke not the truth.
Now, clasping your knees, I implore you by Zeus, aegis-bearer,
Not to condemn me to live as a weakling among mortal men,
But have mercy upon me, for impotence is the lot
Of the unlucky man who lies with an immortal goddess."

The daughter of Zeus, Aphrodite, then answered him, saying:
"Noble Anchises, most glorious of mortal mankind,
Be of good courage and fear not too much in your heart.
You will suffer no evil from me or the other blessed immortals,
For you are dear to the gods, and to you will be born
A son as dear, who will rule over the Trojans
And from whom will descend a line of children to children forever.

The child shall be called Aeneas,* because of my terrible shame
At having fallen into the bed of a mortal,
But those of your race above all of mortal mankind
Forever resemble the gods in beauty and bearing.

"It was because of his beauty that Zeus wise in counsel
Carried off yellow-haired Ganymedes to dwell among the immortals
And in the palace of Zeus to pour out drink for the gods—
A marvel to see, held in honor by all the immortals
As he dips from the golden bowl the rose-colored nectar.
The heart of Tros was filled with unbearable sorrow,
For he knew not whither the whirlwind that came out of heaven
Had taken his son, and he wept for his loss and lamented
Throughout all his days. But Zeus had compassion upon him
And gave him as ransom for Ganymedes high-stepping horses
Such as bear the immortals. These horses he gave
As a gift, and Hermes the Guide, the slayer of Argos,
At the behest of Zeus explained to the father
That the boy, like the gods, would be deathless and free from old age.
Hearing these tidings from Zeus, Tros ceased from lamenting
And with joy in his heart rode with his storm-footed steeds.

"So too was Tithonos, whom gold-enthroned Eos abducted,
Born of your race, like the immortals in beauty.
She went before Zeus, cloud-wrapped son of Cronos, and begged
That her lover be made immortal and live forever.
Zeus nodded his head in assent and fulfilled her desire,
But in her simplicity heavenly Eos neglected
To ask for youth for Tithonos and riddance from grievous old age.
For so long as he bloomed with the lovely vigor of youth
He lived at the ends of the earth by the river of Ocean
Disporting himself with gold-enthroned Eos, daughter of dawn,
But when the first gray showered down and powdered the hair
On his beautiful head and the beard on his nobly carved chin,
Heavenly Eos stayed away from his couch
But sheltered him still in the halls of her palace and served him
Food and ambrosia and gave him fine garments to wear.
When loathsome old age pressed down wholly upon him at last,
No more was he able to move or to raise up his limbs.
Then to the heart of Eos one plan appeared best:
Into an inner chamber she moved him and there laid him down
And shut fast upon him the shining doors. In that haven

* Derived here as if from *ainos* = "terrible."

His voice, indistinct, flows on forever, and no strength remains
Of that earlier power his supple limbs vaunted.
  "Not thus would I take you to be among the immortals
Immortal and, deathless, to live for all time to come.
If you might live out your life just as you are
In form and physique and henceforth be known as my husband,
Pain and distress would not then enfold my grave heart.
But soon now remorseless old age, common to all,
Will enshroud you—age that stands close at hand for all men,
Deadly, wearisome, loathed even by the immortals.
  "But for me there will be great disgrace among the undying gods
For all days forever and ever on your dear account—
They who once feared my taunts and the cunning with which I united
All gods at some time with women of mortal descent,
Subduing them all to my purpose. Never again
Will my tongue wield such power among the immortals,
For I have gone sadly astray; shockingly, blamelessly
Have I gone out of my mind and planted a child
Under my girdle by going to bed with a mortal.
When he is born and first sees the light of the sun,
Deep-breasted mountain-bred nymphs who inhabit this peak,
Lofty and sacred, shall rear him—glorious creatures
Ranking with neither immortals nor mortals.
Long do they live, and they eat of ambrosial food
And glide in the lovely dance among the immortals.
With them the Sileni and the keen-eyed slayer of Argos
Mingle in love in the innermost nooks of delectable caves.
At the time of their birth pine saplings and beautiful oak trees,
High-topped, luxuriant, spring up on the nourishing earth,
Reaching skyward from the slopes of the towering mountains;
So huge do they grow they are called sacred groves of the gods,
And never do mortals fell one with an axe.
But whenever the shadow of death hovers about,
First the great trees wither there on the ground where they stand,
Then the bark flakes away all around and the branches fall off,
And together their souls—nymph and tree—leave behind them
      the light of the sun.
Among them will my son live and be raised.
At the time of the first lovely flowering of very young manhood,
Here will the goddesses bring him and show you your child,
And I myself—to reveal all the things in my heart—

Will return to you in the fifth year leading the boy.
When first you behold your scion with your own eyes
You will rejoice at the sight, for he will be godlike,
And then to windy Troy you will take him at once.
If ever someone of mortal mankind should inquire
What mother carried your dear son under her girdle,
Remember well to tell him what I command you:
Say that the boy was born of a flower-faced nymph,
One of those who inhabit this forest-clad mountain.
If ever you blurt out the truth and foolishly boast
Of having mingled in love with bright-crowned Cytherea,
Zeus in his anger will smite you with a smoldering bolt of swift lightning.
All this I tell you. See to it well in your heart.
Curb your tongue, and never mention my name.
And with awe and reverence fear the wrath of the gods."
 Speaking thus, Aphrodite ascended to high, windy heaven.
 Farewell, goddess, you who stand guard over well-founded Cyprus;
With a hymn to you I began, and I will move on to another.

· 6 · To Aphrodite ·

BEAUTIFUL golden-crowned Aphrodite, goddess adored,
    I will sing, who has for her share the walls of all Cyprus
    Set in the sea, where the moist breath of Zephyros blowing
        Out of the west bore her over the surge of the loud-roaring deep
In soft foam. The gold-filleted Hours
Welcomed her gladly and clothed her in ambrosial garments
And on her immortal head set a chaplet of richly wrought gold.
Flowerlike earrings formed of fine brass and rare gold
They fastened then in Aphrodite's pierced ear lobes,
And around her delicate throat and silvery breasts
Hung necklaces inlaid with gold, of the sort
The gold-filleted Hours themselves wear when they go
To the lovely dance of the gods and the house of their father.
When they had wholly arrayed the goddess in splendor,
They led her to the immortals, who, seeing her, welcomed her kindly
And offered their right hands in greeting. Amazed by the beauty
Of violet-crowned Cytherea, every god prayed
To lead her as his lawful wife to his home.
    Farewell, gentle goddess whose sidelong glance sweetly entices:
Grant that in this contest I be the victor and urge on my lay.
But I will remember you and another song too.

· 7 · To Dionysos ·

DIONYSOS, son of most glorious Semele, will I remember:
How he appeared on a headland jutting out over the sand
On the shore of the unfruitful sea, seeming in form like a youth
In the first flower of manhood. His rich mane of dark hair
Floated about him in beauty, and over his sturdy shoulders
He wore a mantle of purple. Over the wine-dark water
Men, Tyrsenian pirates, swiftly approached in a vessel
Well banked with oars, led to that spot by an evil fate.
At sight of the god, the pirates nodded one to another
And quickly leaped from their ship and seized him straightway
And forced him aboard, their hearts filled with rejoicing.
They thought him a prince, a son of god-cherished kings,
And sought to bind him fast hand and foot with tight fetters.
But bonds would not hold him; from hands and feet the strands fell away
And lay scattered about far and wide on the deck,
While the god sat, a smile lurking in his dark eyes.
The helmsman alone understood, and called out at once to his shipmates:
    "Fools, what powerful god is this you have taken and fettered?
Our ship, strongly built as it is, cannot carry him!
This must be Zeus, or the god of the silver bow, lord Apollo,
Or Poseidon perhaps, for he is not like a mortal
But like the gods who have their homes on Olympus.
Come, let us at once set him free upon the dark mainland.
Lay not your hands upon him lest in his anger
He should let loose upon us strong winds and a terrible tempest!"
    So he spoke, but the captain, chiding him, sneeringly answered:
"Idiot! Look to the wind and hoist up the sail of the ship,
Hauling on all sheets together! As for this one,
We men will see to him. He's bound, I would venture, for Egypt
Or Cyprus or north to the Hyperboreans, or yet even farther away.
In the end he will tell us about his friends and relations
And all his possessions, since fate has cast him among us."
    So he spoke, and the mast was stepped and the sail of the ship
        was run up

55

And the wind blew and bellied the sail, and the sailors stretched taut
The rigging, securing it well on each side. All of a sudden
Wonders and marvels began to appear all around them.
Wine, first of all, fragrant and sweet to the taste,
Murmurously flowed throughout the swift-sailing black ship
And a heavenly odor perfumed the air. Amazement
Seized the hearts of all seamen who saw it. Then in an instant
A vine, running along the topmost edge of the sail,
Sprang up and sent out its branches in every direction
Heavy with thick-hanging clusters of grapes, and around the mast
Curled dark-leaved ivy, rich in blossoms and bright with ripe berries,
And garlands crowned every tholepin. Wild-eyed, the sailors
Entreated the helmsman to guide the ship in to shore,
But within the ship the god turned himself into a lion,
Loudly roaring and menacing in the extreme.
Then as a sign of his might the god made to appear
A bear shaggy of neck, who reared up raging amidship,
While in the peak of the bow the lion still glared baleful-eyed.
The sailors in terror fled to the stern of the ship
And, senseless with fear, gathered about their sure-minded helmsman.
The lion suddenly sprang at the captain and seized him
As the sailors looked on, and all, to escape a like evil fate,
Leapt from the ship into the shining salt sea
And were changed into dolphins. But toward the good helmsman the god
Dionysos showed mercy, and him he held back and addressed
With a brief word, making him blessedly happy:

"Courage, good fellow! I am well pleased with you in my heart.
Dionysos of the loud shout am I; the mother who bore me
To Zeus of their union in love was Semele, daughter of Cadmos."

Farewell, child of lovely-eyed Semele. Never at all
Can he who forgets you find how to order sweet song.

· 8 · To Ares ·

ARES, surpassing in strength, gold-helmeted burden of chariots,
   Hard-headed shield-bearing guardian of cities clad in bronze
      armor,
         Strong of arm and unwearying, skilled with the spear, bulwark
of Olympus,
Father of battle-wise Victory, joined in alliance with Themis,
Tyrant of those who oppose force with force, commander of right-
      minded men,
Bearer of the scepter of manhood, whirling your fiery disk
Through the ether among the seven tracks of the heavenly bodies,
Where above the third orbit your spirited horses forever uphold you,
Hear me, helper of mortals, dispenser of youthful courage!
Shower down into my life from on high your soft radiance
And warlike strength that I may drive bitter evil away from my head
And subdue in my breast my soul's fraudulent passions.
Blunt too the sharp fury of temper that stirs and provokes me
To tread the chill pathway of combat. Instead, blessed one,
Give me the courage to live in the safe ways of peace,
Shunning strife and ill will and the violent fiends of destruction.

· 9 · To Artemis ·

SING, Muse, of Artemis, sister of the Far-Darter,
Virgin delighting in arrows, born and reared with Apollo.
She waters her horses in Meles, deep-grown with rushes,
And drives her solid-gold chariot swiftly through Smyrna
To vine-rich Claros, where Apollo with bow of silver
Sits awaiting the far-shooting goddess delighting in arrows.
Thus with my song I hail you, and all other goddesses too.
I have started to sing first of all about you and yours,
And, beginning with you, will turn now to a hymn to another.

· 10 · To Aphrodite ·

I WILL sing in praise of Cyprus-born Cytherea,
    Who bestows gentle gifts upon mortals, and whose lovely face
    Ever smiles. Lovely, too, the flight of the blushes upon it.
    Hail, goddess, guardian of strongly built Salamis
And of Cyprus set in the sea! Grant that my song be enchanting.
But I will remember you and another song too.

· 11 · To Athene ·

I SING of Pallas Athene, the city's protectress,
  Awesome, and jointly with Ares attendant on matters of warfare—
  The plunder of cities, the loud battle shout, and the fighting—
Who keeps safe from all harm the host going forth and returning
from combat.
  Hail, goddess, and grant to us happiness and good fortune!

· 12 · To Hera ·

GOLDEN-THRONED Hera I sing, daughter of Rhea,
Queen of immortals, surpassing all others in beauty,
Sister and wife of loud-thundering Zeus, glorious goddess
Whom all the blessed gods sheltered by lofty Olympus
Reverence and equally honor with Zeus whose delight is in thunder.

· 13 · To Demeter ·

AWESOME divinity, bright-haired Demeter, I sing to begin,
Her and her daughter Persephone, fairest of maidens.
Hail, goddess! Keep safe this city and govern my song!

· 14 · To the Mother of the Gods ·

SING to me, Muse, clear-voiced daughter of powerful Zeus,
  Of the mother of all the gods and of all mankind,
  Who delights in drums and the rattle of castanets,
    The wailing of pipes, the howling of wolves, and the fierce lion's roar,
And in all the echoing hills and tree-shadowed valleys.
    Thus with my song I greet you, and all other goddesses too.

· 15 · To Heracles the Lion-Hearted ·

HERACLES will I sing, son of Olympian Zeus,
Strongest by far of men who inhabit the earth,
Born to Alcmene in Thebes, city of beautiful dances,
Of her union in love with black-clouded Zeus son of Cronos.
In earlier times he roamed the unmeasured expanse
Of land and sea at the will of Eurystheus the king;
Many were the dangerous tasks he performed and much did he suffer,
But now in the lovely abode of snow-capped Olympus
He joyously lives with slim-ankled Hebe, his wife.
    Hail, lord, son of Zeus; grant with prosperity excellence!

· 16 · To Asclepios ·

PHYSICIAN of illness, Asclepios, son of Apollo,
 In the beginning I sing, born on the Dotian plain
 To shining Coronis, daughter of Phlegyas the king,
 To mankind a great joy, who charms away painful affliction.
Thus, lord, I hail you, and with my singing entreat you.

· 17 · To the Dioscuri ·

SING, clear-voiced Muse, of Castor and Polydeuces,
Tyndaridae, sons begotten by Olympian Zeus,
Born under the crown of Taÿgetos, Leda, their mother,
Unwittingly having yielded in love to the cloud-wreathed
son of Cronos.
    Hail, Tyndaridae, riders of swift-footed horses!

· 18 · To Hermes ·

I SING Cyllenian Hermes, slayer of Argos,
   Guardian over Cyllene and sheep-rich Arcadia,
   Helpful messenger of the immortals, whom Maia,
   Daughter of Atlas, bore to Zeus of their union in love.
Modestly shunning the throng of the blessed immortals,
She lived in a shadowy cave, where Zeus son of Cronos
Lay with the lovely-haired nymph in the deep of the night
When sweet sleep possessed white-armed Hera, escaping thereby
The observance of undying gods and of mortal mankind.
   Thus do I greet you, son of Zeus and of Maia.
After beginning with you, I move on to a hymn to another.
Farewell, grace-giving Hermes, Conductor, bestower of blessings!

· 19 · To Pan ·

S PEAK to me, Muse, of the son beloved of Hermes,
   Goat-footed, two-horned lover of noisy confusion,
   Who cavorts through the woodland dells with the dancing nymphs—
   They who lightly tread the steep rocky cliffs that are shunned
Even by goats, calling aloud to the shepherd god Pan,
Bright-haired and disheveled, who has for his share every snow-covered
      ridge,
The towering summits of mountains, and sheer rock-slabbed steeps.
Hither and thither through the dense thickets he wanders,
Now drawn from his course by gently murmuring streams,
Now clambering over high rocky cliffs, ascending
The uttermost peak that stands watch over flocks as they graze.
Often he runs through the lofty white-shining mountains
And often over the slopes in the chase, keen-eyed and alert,
Killing wild beasts. Home from the hunt returning at evening
He sounds his lonely note, playing sweet songs
On his pipes of reed. Not even that bird can surpass him in song
Who in blossoming springtime pours forth her lament
From her leafy bower, grieving in honey-sweet tones.
Then the clear-caroling nymphs of the mountain who wander
The woodland lightfooted with Pan sing by a spring of black water,
And about the high peak of the mountain Echo resounds.
The god glides in and out in the dance, on this side and that,
Now prancing on nimble feet in the very midst of the chorus,
Wearing the tawny pelt of a lynx on his shoulders,
His heart exulting in music's shrill sweetness there in the soft meadow
Where, tangled in grass, crocus and sweet-smelling hyacinth bloom
      intermingled.
   The blessed gods they hymn, and lofty Olympus,
And they sing of luck-bringing Hermes above all the others:
How he as swift messenger serves all the gods,
And how he arrived in Arcadia, land rich in fountains,
Mother of flocks, where lies his sacred precinct Cyllene.
There though a god he tended a flock of shaggy-fleeced sheep

In the hire of a mortal, for tender longing came of a sudden
Upon him and grew, to lie united in love
With the daughter of Dryops, nymph with beautiful tresses,
And he brought to pass the felicitous marriage. Dryope
Bore in the women's halls of the palace a dear son to Hermes,
From the beginning a marvelous sight to behold:
Goat-footed, two-horned, delighting in noise, gaily laughing.
The nurse, when she looked on his hideous face, fully bearded,
Sprang up and fled from the baby, sorely afraid.
But luck-bringing Hermes, receiving his son, at once
Took him into his arms, his heart filled with joy beyond measure,
And swiftly he went to the seat of the undying gods
With the child warmly wrapped in the skins of mountain-bred hares,
And laid him down beside Zeus and presented his son to the other
　　immortals.
All the undying gods rejoiced in their hearts,
But Bacchic Dionysos beyond all the rest,
And they called him Pan,* because he delighted all hearts.
　　Thus, lord, farewell; with my song I appease you,
But I will remember you and other songs too.

* Derived here as if from *pas* = "all."

· 20 · To Hephaistos ·

SING, clear-voiced Muse, of Hephaistos, renowned for his skill,
   Who with gray-eyed Athene taught to men upon earth
   Arts of great splendor, men who in former days lived
      Like wild beasts in caves in the mountains. But having learned skills
From Hephaistos, famed for his craft, they now, free from care,
Tranquilly live out their lives year by year in their houses.
   Be gracious, Hephaistos, and excellence grant with your bounty!

· 21 · To Apollo ·

YOU, Phoebus, even the swan sings with its shrill cry
    Under its wings as it lights on the bank by the eddying river
    Peneios, and you the bard holding the clear-sounding phorminx
    Ever sings in his sweet voice both first and last.
Thus, lord, I greet you, and with my song seek your favor.

· 22 · To Poseidon ·

I BEGIN by singing about the great god Poseidon,
  Mighty mover of earth and the unfruitful sea,
  Lord of the deep, who rules over Helicon * and far-reaching Aegae.
The gods, Earth-Shaker, allotted to you a double distinction:
To be both the tamer of horses and the preserver of ships.
  Hail, Poseidon, dark-haired Upholder of Earth!
Keep a compassionate heart, blessed one, and help those who sail.

* I.e., Helike.

· 23 · To the Most High, the Son of Cronos ·

ZEUS, the greatest and best of the gods, I will sing,
Far-seeing ruler who brings all things to fulfillment
And holds wise discourse with Themis, who sits nearby
leaning toward him.
Be gracious, far-seeing one, son of Cronos, noblest and greatest!

· 24 · To Hestia ·

HESTIA, you who attend the holy house of Apollo,
Far-Darter, in sanctified Pytho, you from whose hair
Drips forever moist scented oil, draw near this dwelling.
Come, goddess of one mind with Zeus wise in counsel,
And bestow on my song at the same time your blessing.

· 25 · To the Muses and Apollo ·

I WOULD begin with the Muses, Apollo, and Zeus,
For because of the Muses and the Far-Shooter, Apollo,
Men there are on earth who are bards and who play on the lyre.
But kings are from Zeus. Happy is he who is loved by the Muses;
Sweet flows the voice from out of his mouth.
Hail, children of Zeus, and honor my song!
But I will remember you and another song too.

· 26 · To Dionysos ·

IVY-WREATHED Dionysos of the loud shout I sing,
　Radiant son of Zeus and all-glorious Semele,
　Nurtured by lovely-haired nymphs who, receiving the child
　　From the lord his father, took him to their breasts and tenderly
reared him
In the grottoes of Nysa. There, in a sweet-smelling cave,
He lived among the nymphs by the will of his father,
Growing in strength and numbered among the immortals.
But after the nymphs had raised the god everywhere honored
In hymns, he wandered at will through the wooded dells,
His brow enwreathed with ivy and laurel, the nymphs
Following after, their outcry resounding throughout the vast woodland.
　Thus do I hail you, Dionysos, heavy with clusters.
Grant that we return to this season rejoicing,
And from this season on again through the many years.

· 27 · To Artemis ·

ARTEMIS I sing, of the arrow of gold and the hunting cry,
  Chaste virgin pursuing the deer, showering arrows,
  Own sister of gold-bladed Apollo, who courses
  Over the shadowy hills and wind-swept peaks
Taking delight in the chase, and, bending her golden bow,
Sends forth her arrows of anguish. The peaks of the high mountains
    tremble,
And the shady woodland screams with the cries of wild creatures;
Earth itself shudders, and the deep sea teeming with fish,
As the brave goddess turns this way and that, slaying the race of
    wild beasts.
But when the showerer of arrows is sated with searching for game
And her heart is content, she slackens the well-bent bow
And goes to the great house of her dear brother, Phoebus Apollo,
In the rich land of Delphi, and orders the beautiful dance of the
    Muses and Graces.
There, hanging up her curve-backed bow and her quiver of arrows,
Her figure adorned in elegant raiment, she takes command
And leads in the dances. They all raise their heavenly voices
In hymns of praise to Leto, delicate-ankled,
Telling in song of how she gave birth to children
Foremost in counsel and deeds among the immortals.
  Farewell, children of Zeus and of lovely-haired Leto;
I will remember you both and another song too.

· 28 · To Athene ·

PALLAS ATHENE, glorious goddess, I sing to begin,
   Gray-eyed divinity ever ready with counsel, steadfast of heart,
   Virgin revered, guarding the city, mighty in valor,
      Born on the shore of Tritonis, where Zeus wise in counsel
Himself gave birth to the goddess from out of his own august head.
She came forth accoutered for warfare in glistening gold,
An awesome sight to all the other immortals.
Springing vigorous from the immortal head,
She stood proudly arrayed before Zeus, aegis-bearer,
And brandished her spear. Great Olympus itself started to reel,
Dazed by the might of the gray-eyed newcomer, and earth all around
Cried out in fear, while the sea heaved, throwing up
Purple billows and spewing forth sudden foam.
The brilliant son of Hyperion halted his swift-footed horses,
Forgetful of time, until the maid Pallas Athene
Stripped from her immortal shoulders her armor divine,
And gladness brightened the face of Zeus wise in counsel.
   Thus do I hail you, daughter of Zeus, aegis-bearer;
But I will remember you and another song too.

· 29 · To Hestia ·

HESTIA, you who of all in the lofty halls
  Of immortal gods and of men who walk on the earth
  Obtained a home everlasting and highest honor,
    Beautiful is your prize, and precious, for without you
No feasts would there be for mortals, where first and last
An offering of honey-sweet wine is poured out to Hestia.
And you, slayer of Argos, son of Zeus and of Maia,
Gold-wanded messenger of the blessed immortals,
Giver of good things, be gracious and come to my aid,
Joining with Hestia, goddess reverenced and dear.
Dwell here in this noble house with love in your hearts for each other,
And both being mindful of men who live upon earth
And of their fine deeds, urge on their efforts with vigor.
    Farewell, daughter of Cronos, and you, gold-wanded Hermes.
But I will remember you both and another song too.

· 30 · To Earth, Mother of All ·

GAIA, mother of all, I sing, oldest of gods,
Firm of foundation, who feeds all creatures living on earth,
As many as move on the radiant land and swim in the sea
And fly through the air—all these does she feed with her bounty.
Mistress, from you come our fine children and bountiful harvests;
Yours is the power to give mortals life and to take it away.
Happy is he upon whom your glance falls with favor,
Finding him worthy; to him come all things in abundance.
His life-giving acres of cornland at harvest are heavily laden,
Cattle abound in his pastures, his house is filled with good things.
Such rule in order their city of beautiful women,
Great happiness attendant upon them, and wealth.
Their sons, overflowing with youthful high spirits, exult,
And their maidenly daughters in flowery bands, happily playing,
Skip through the delicate blossoms that blow in the meadows.
These do you honor, goddess most holy, bounteous spirit.
   Hail to you, mother of gods, wife of starry Uranos!
Graciously grant for my song means for the life I desire.
But I will remember you and another song too.

· 31 · To Helios ·

BEGIN, Muse, Calliope, daughter of Zeus, once more to sing
  Of Helios, brilliantly shining, whom velvet-eyed Euryphaëssa
  Bore to the son of Gaia and starry Uranos.
    For Hyperion married his sister, all-glorious Euryphaëssa,
And she bore him beautiful children—rosy-armed Eos,
Lovely, rich-haired Selene, and untiring Helios
Like the immortals, who shines upon men and undying gods
As he drives his swift chariot. His eyes blindingly flash
From under his helmet of gold, and dazzling rays glitter
Around his brow, and the bright hair that gracefully flows
Down from his head conceals his far-shining face.
His splendid fine-woven garment shimmers about him
And flutters in the breath of the winds as he drives with his stallions.
Then, halting his golden-yoked chariot and horses, he rests
There at the highest summit of heaven, awaiting the moment
To drive back again, more than mortal, through heaven to Ocean.
    Hail, lord, and graciously grant me a suitable living!
With you I began, and now I will extol
The race of earthborn men blessed with speech, demi-gods,
Whose deeds the heavenly Muses have made known to mortals.

· 32 · To Selene ·

TELL of the wide-winged moon, O Muses, sweet-voiced
Daughters of Zeus son of Cronos, you who are well-versed
in song.
    The light from her immortal head flows down from heaven
And bathes all the earth, and under her shining glory
Great beauty emerges. The sky, dark without her,
Grows bright from the glow of her golden crown, and her rays
    fill the air
Whenever, after bathing her lovely body, shining Selene
Arises from Ocean and dons her garments that gleam from afar,
When she yokes together her glistening colts with high-arching necks
And drives her team, glossy-coated, impetuously forward
At eventide at the full of the moon. Her great pathway then is complete;
Her beams at that time of waxing shine brightest from heaven,
And she is revealed as a sign and a token to mortals.
    Once in the bed of love the son of Cronos lay with her,
And she conceived and gave birth to the maiden Pandea,
Outstanding in beauty among the gods everlasting.
    Hail, queen, snowy-armed goddess, shining Selene,
Benign, lovely-haired! With you I have begun,
And now I will sing the glory of men semi-divine
Whose exploits minstrels serving the Muses extol with mellifluous voices.

· 33 · To the Dioscuri ·

GLANCING-EYED Muses, tell of the twin sons of Zeus,
Tyndaridae, glorious children of slim-ankled Leda,
Castor the tamer of horses and Polydeuces the blameless,
Born to her under the summit of Taÿgetos' towering height
Of her union in love with black-clouded Zeus son of Cronos—
Children born to be saviors of men upon earth
And of swift-sailing ships when winter's gales
Rage over the unsparing sea. The sailors then, praying,
Call on the sons of great Zeus and offer white lambs,
Crowding together up to the high end of the stern.
But the strong wind and the sea's mountainous waves
Drive the ship under. Then suddenly the twin brothers appear,
Darting on tawny wings through the sky, and at once
Still the blasts of the turbulent gale and quiet
The tossing surge of white foam on the face of the sea—
A favorable sign of freedom from toil for sailors,
Who rejoice at the sight and rest from their arduous labor.
　　Farewell, Tyndaridae, riders of swift-footed horses!
Yet you and another song too will I remember.